100 • FAST
NOODLES

100·FAST NOODLES

JOHN MIDGLEY

PAVILION

for Sue

First published in Great Britain in 1995 by
Pavilion Books Limited
26 Upper Ground
London SE1 9PD

Text copyright © 1995 by John Midgley
The moral right of the author has been asserted
Illustrations copyright © 1995 by Andrew Farmer
Cover photograph © 1995 by James Murphy

Designed by Elizabeth Ayer

A CIP catalogue record for this book is available from the British Library

ISBN 1-85793-573 X
Typeset in ITC Garamond

10 9 8 7 6 5 4 3 2 1

This book may be ordered by post direct from the publisher.
Please contact the Marketing Department. But try your bookshop first.

Printed and bound in Great Britain by
Butler & Tanner Ltd, Frome and London

CONTENTS

Cold noodle dishes and noodle salads *55*

Stir-fried and deep-fried noodle dishes 75

Noodle curries *119*

INTRODUCTION

Noodles made with wheat and rice flours have been eaten in China for well over 2000 years, and are very rapidly gaining popularity in the West. Opinion remains divided as to their place and period of origin. Some say China, others Etruscan Italy, ancient Greece, the Middle East, or Russia. In any event, noodles and pasta have long co-existed, whether or not they were invented separately.

Like Italian pasta, Oriental noodles are the fast food *par excellence*, but they are even more versatile. As this book demonstrates, noodles are the basis of wonderful soups, cold and warm salads, spicy stir-fries and fragrant curries. Although the preparation time of the ingredients that accompany them can be relatively lengthy, the actual cooking time is almost invariably minimal, and many recipes are cooked in under five minutes.

Oriental noodles are generally rather different in texture from pasta and other European noodles. Most varieties are softer and starchier than pasta, which is made from hard durum wheat flour. One kind, however, made not from flour but from mung bean starch, is decidedly slippery, and is perhaps an acquired taste for some people. Rice noodles and cellophane noodles are especially delicious deep-fried. On contact with the hot oil they instantly puff up into a feather-light, crisp nimbus, making a delightful nest for a variety of spicy, saucy toppings. It is rewarding to experiment with different versions.

Most Oriental noodles are readily available in both their fresh and dried forms. Chinese, Thai and Japanese supermarkets and food shops usually stock both, but the fresh ones are rarely labelled and even then, not in English. Your best bet in identifying fresh noodles is to consult a cookery book that includes colour photographs of ingredients. Or ask the staff!

Fortunately for those who live far from those excellent ethnic establishments, the main supermarket chains stock dried egg noodles, which in most cases can be substituted for the other varieties specified in the recipes. Sainsbury's initiative to introduce rare and exotic ingredients into their main branches means that you will now also find buckwheat *soba* noodles and a wide range of complementary Japanese ingredients such as dried seaweed (for *dashi* stock), *wasabi*, soy bean paste, dark sesame oil, *mirin* and *sake* (rice wine), rice vinegar, dried shiitake mushrooms, bonito shavings, and sansho pepper.

All dried noodles and some fresh ones need boiling in unsalted water until *al dente*. (It is advisable to check the packet instructions when boiling dried noodles.) Some fresh noodles, such as Chinese 'oil' noodles, are sold pre-cooked. They are usually added to soups and stir-fried together with shredded meat and vegetables.

These are the most commonly available noodle varieties, and are the ones referred to in the subsequent recipes.

Egg Noodles

Egg noodles are made with wheat flour,
water and eggs and come in several
different forms, from round noodles to flat
ribbons, of varying thicknesses. Their
colours range from yellowy-orange
through bright yellow to pale buff. They
are hugely popular in China, wherever
there are Chinese communities, and in
Japan, where they are called *ramen*.

Dried egg noodles should be cooked
according to the packet instructions, and if
in tight nests, should be stirred while they
boil to disentangle the strands. When *al
dente* they should be rinsed under cold
water to prevent them from sticking
together, drained, and unless used quickly,
it is a good idea to toss them in a little oil
to be sure of loose, separate strands.

Fresh egg noodles are sold packaged in
clear plastic bags and may be found in the
refrigerated section of Chinese supermarkets. They need much less boiling than
dried egg noodles – most should be *al
dente* after just a minute or two. Fresh egg
noodles freeze very well, so if you can
only obtain them occasionally, it is worth
buying several packets. Either leave the
frozen noodles out to thaw naturally or
remove them from the bag and cook in
boiling water, allowing a little extra time.

Fresh egg 'oil' noodles are pre-cooked
and can go straight into the wok for
stir-frying. You will recognize them by
their oily texture and thick, round strands.
They are the noodles that I like best for
spicy stir-fries and curries.

Dried egg noodles, boiled until *al
dente*, can usually be successfully
substituted for fresh. As a rule of thumb,
for 450g/1lb fresh noodles allow 225g/8oz
dried – a little less if very thin.

Rice noodles

These are just as varied as egg noodles,
and may sometimes be obtained fresh but
are widely available dried. Thin, dried rice
noodles are often labelled 'rice sticks' or,
if very thin, 'rice vermicelli', and are
excellent in soups and salads, stir-fries
and curries. Rice 'vermicelli' are perfect
for deep-frying, instantly puffing up and
turning crisp and light. Broad, ribbon rice
noodles are particularly popular in Thailand
and China. Dried rice noodles are very
starchy and should be treated in the same
way as dried egg noodles after boiling.

Fresh rice noodles are made from rice
flour, water and wheat starch; dried ones
just from rice flour and water. The fresh
rice noodles that you are most likely to
find are white and thick, either round or
flat and ribbon-like. They do not freeze
well and are highly perishable. They are,
however, delicious, as long as they are not
overcooked.

Wheat noodles

Made from wheat flour and water, most
Oriental wheat noodles are of Japanese or
Chinese origin. These are the principal
varieties:

Somen noodles

Very thin, round, white Japanese noodles. I have only ever found dried *somen*, usually beautifully packaged in cellophane and tied in neat little bundles bound by a ribbon or paper band. They cook very quickly, usually in under 2 minutes, and are best in soups and soupy dishes.

Udon noodles

Thick, round or flat, white Japanese noodles, available both fresh and dried. Prepared as above, the fresh ones need little if any cooking. They are especially delicious in soupy or saucy dishes. Cook the dried ones as directed on the packet instructions. If these are unintelligible allow 3–5 minutes' boiling but check periodically for tenderness.

Kishimen noodles

Thick, flat, white Japanese noodles, similar to, and interchangeable with, *udon* noodles.

Buckwheat noodles *(soba)*

Buckwheat is in fact entirely unrelated to wheat, and is not even classified as a grain. Buckwheat has been important in Japanese cuisine for many hundreds of years, especially in the form of *soba* noodles. Thin, round, and either brownish-grey, pale buff, or off-white in colour, they are rarely available fresh, but dried ones are quite easily obtained. *Soba* noodles are served both hot and chilled, the latter accompanied by dipping sauce. The best *soba* are sweetish, with a refreshing flavour.

There is also a variety called tea *soba* or *cha soba*, in which buckwheat noodles are flavoured with green tea.

Mung bean noodles (cellophane noodles)

Also known as bean thread noodles and glass noodles, cellophane noodles are made from ground mung beans. They are white and brittle in dried form and, when soaked in hot water for about 15 minutes, soften to a strange, slippery texture, becoming transparent. Most mung bean noodles come from China.

All dried noodles store very well in a cool, dry, preferably dark place, and are thus excellent storecupboard ingredients. Fresh noodles may be kept refrigerated for three or four days, although fresh rice noodles will only keep for 24–48 hours.

OTHER INGREDIENTS USED

These are some of the less common ingredients referred to in the recipes. By no means rare, many will be found in the larger supermarkets, but some may need to be sought out in specialist food shops or obtained by mail order.

Alfalfa sprouts

Similar to, but much smaller and finer than the more commonly available sprouted mung beans, these are nutty and delicious, packed full of protein and minerals.

Aubergines (eggplant)

There are many different kinds of aubergines: tiny pea aubergines; round varieties resembling tomatoes; long, slender ones; and the more familiar large, purple aubergines. They come in a variety of colours – white, yellow, green, and purple, and some are variegated or streaky. Look for very firm ones with bright, shiny skins. Small, immature aubergines are not at all seedy and bitter, and so do not need purging with salt.

Baby corn

This is sweetcorn that is harvested while immature, and is a an ideal vegetable for eating lightly cooked or raw. The cobs can be white or pale yellow.

Bamboo shoots

The edible shoots of certain bamboo varieties. Look in Chinese supermarkets for bamboo shoots preserved in brine or buy the canned ones, which are usually ready-sliced.

Basil, sweet, holy

Sweet basil is the familiar, large-leaved aromatic herb recently popularized by the vogue for Mediterranean food. All supermarkets sell it year-round, whether as pot plants or harvested and packaged in cellophane bags. Holy basil is an altogether spicier-smelling herb with smaller leaves and lovely purple flowers. It grows as a weed in Thailand but, surprisingly, thrives in temperate climates in good summers. It is hard to obtain but very easily grown from seed.

Bean curd

Also known as *tofu*, bean curd is an ancient product of soy beans. The soft, creamy variety is sometimes called 'silken *tofu*', and is best in soups, whereas the solid variety called for in the recipes that follow stands up well to stir-frying. Supermarkets sell bean curd packed in small, vacuum-packed cardboard cartons, but the fresh kind will be found floating in water in plastic trays in the refrigerated section of Chinese supermarkets. Store bean curd blocks in a refrigerated tray of water, change the water daily and they should keep for up to four days.

Bean sauce, yellow, brown

Made from fermented soy beans, these thick, commercially-made sauces give an unmistakably spicy, savoury flavour to Chinese dishes.

Bean sprouts

These thick, crisp, white sprouts of mung beans are indispensable in noodle cuisine, featuring in many of the recipes. Best added raw as a garnish or towards the end of the cooking, bean sprouts are highly nutritious and delightfully crunchy. They are widely available year-round but should be used up quickly. Never use canned bean sprouts, which are soggy.

Black beans
Sold in plastic bags, dried, fermented black beans are quite salty and should be rinsed before cooking. They are best chopped or mashed.

Bonito flakes, dried (han-katsuo)
A relative of tuna, bonito is a popular fish species in Japan. Dried fillets are shaved to produce flakes which are sold in plastic bags. Bonito flakes or shavings are an essential ingredient in Japanese *dashi* (stock).

Cayenne
Cayenne is the powdered product of ground, hot cayenne peppers. Ordinary chili powder (not American chili powder, which is a spice mixture containing ground cumin and oregano) may be substituted for cayenne.

Chilies; dried red, fresh red and green, Thai bird's-eye, chili flakes
Chili peppers are widely used throughout Asia. There are hundreds of varieties, but as a rule of thumb, the smaller the pepper the hotter it will be. Tiny Thai bird's-eyes are among the hottest. Fresh and dried chilies are always available, the latter on the spice shelves of supermarkets and in Indian and Chinese food shops. Chili flakes are whole dried red chilies reduced to flakes, seeds and all.

Chili bean sauce
This Chinese sauce sold in little jars is usually a mixture in which fermented soy beans, chilies, garlic and seasonings predominate. It can be very hot and pungent and should be added sparingly to stir-fry sauces.

Chili oil
Dried red chilies of varying degrees of heat steeped in peanut or other vegetable oil produce a seasoning that is added very sparingly to all manner of dishes, and also used as a dipping condiment.

Chili sauce
The best bottled brands are Chinese but chili sauces are popular throughout Asia. Chilies, vinegar and plums are the main ingredients. Chili sauce is smoother and runnier than chili bean sauce.

Chinese leaf cabbage
Also called Chinese celery cabbage, this vegetable looks like a cross between a Cos (romaine) lettuce and a white cabbage. It is excellent raw and lightly stir-fried, with a good crunchy texture. Not to be confused with (though in fact sometimes

interchangeable with) *pak choy* or Chinese white cabbage.

Coconut milk

Canned coconut milk (unsweetened) is available in both Chinese and national supermarkets. Unless well shaken or mixed, the thick 'cream' and thin watery liquid will have separated. Thai and Malaysian brands are excellent.

Coriander (cilantro)

Fresh coriander, which is sometimes called Chinese parsley, looks a little like flat-leaf parsley but it has a warm, spicy, orangey aroma. The roots are commonly incorporated in south-east Asian curry pastes, and the leaves are an ubiquitous garnish throughout Asia.

Curry pastes: Thai 'red', Thai 'green', green 'masala', Indian

Although best freshly made, commercial curry pastes are a boon to the busy cook, and are available in both Oriental and national supermarkets. I do not hesitate to use them in noodle curries.

Curry powder

The same comments apply, although some curry powders are already stale when sold, contain a disproportionate amount of ground turmeric, and if used in large quantities mask the taste of the ingredients you are cooking.

Dashi granules

Instant *dashi* is possible with these granules. However, they do contain monosodium glutamate so avoid if you have suffered from 'Chinese restaurant syndrome' symptoms! Available by mail order (see page 141).

Dried kelp (konbu)

The dark green, folded flat sheets of giant kelp are an essential ingredient in Japanese *dashi*. Wipe but do not wash as the white 'bloom' is where the flavour resides. *Konbu* should simmer gently until it starts to soften but boiling produces an unpleasant smell. Available in some good food halls, in Japanese shops and by mail order.

Fish sauce

Ubiquitous throughout south-east Asia and the Far East, fish sauce is the thin, brown, salty and savoury liquid produced from salted and fermented fish, shrimp or squid. It is called *nam pla* in Thailand, *patis* in the Philippines and *nuoc mam* in Vietnam. Until recently only available in Oriental supermarkets and food shops, fish sauce is now stocked by the larger supermarket branches. Many of the recipes require fish sauce, for which there is no substitute. There are quite a few recipes containing no fish or meat but which are flavoured with fish sauce. Strict vegetarians may substitute soy sauce.

Galangal

A rhizome related to ginger, fresh galangal is highly perfumed and is much used in Thai and south-east Asian dishes. Although available in both fresh and dried forms in Oriental supermarkets, the fresh is much preferred.

Garam masala

A popular Indian mixture of ground 'heating' spices, usually containing black peppercorns, cumin and coriander seeds, cloves, cinnamon, cardamom, etc. *Garam masala* is best made up at home in small quantities as it loses fragrance quickly, and commercial brands can be stale.

Ginger

An aromatic rhizome that is used all over the world, but especially in Asian cuisines, ginger is widely available in both fresh and powdered forms. One of the four or five essential ingredients in Chinese cooking.

Hoisin sauce

A thick, dark, sweet bottled or canned sauce that is widely used in Chinese cooking. It is sometimes called 'barbecue sauce', and is available in the larger supermarket branches and also Oriental supermarkets and food shops.

Japanese noodle broth concentrate

Generally of good quality, when diluted this concentrate makes light work of any noodle dishes requiring *dashi*. It is also used in a less diluted form for Japanese dipping sauces. Available in large or small bottles resembling soy sauce, from Muji and other Japanese shops, and also by mail order (see page 141).

Japanese 7-spice mixture *(schichimi)*

A delicious addition to Japanese noodle dishes, the seven ground spices are: red pepper, brown *sansho* pods, dried mandarin orange peel, hemp seeds, white poppy seeds, *nori* seaweed, white sesame seeds.

Kaffir lime leaves

The kaffir or wild lime, produces a knobbly fruit that is much valued for its aromatic, zesty rind. The leaves also have a wonderful flavour and perfume that characterize many Thai and south-east Asian dishes. They are available in Oriental shops in both fresh and dried forms, and are usually snipped into thin strips before being added to the other ingredients.

Lemon grass

A tropical grass that may be grown under glass in temperate climates. Fresh lemon grass is available in Oriental supermarkets and also in some of the larger national supermarkets. Dried strips and powdered lemon grass are also available though not as good. The flavour and scent are delightful and hard to replicate. Strip off the outer

leaves and trim off the tougher parts
of the stalk. Finely slice the tender
part remaining.

'Little gem' lettuce

A deliciously sweet, crisp lettuce related to
the Cos (romaine), and a good substitute
for lettuce hearts. The whole lettuce may
be used. 'Little gem' is widely available in
supermarkets.

Lime

A juicy tropical citrus with a distinctive
perfume and flavour. Small, smooth and
green in appearance, cultivated limes are
not to be confused with the aforemen-
tioned kaffir limes. Lemon juice and rind
may be substituted.

Mint

Although there are many varieties, both
wild and cultivated, spearmint is the most
popular. Mint is commonly used in dried
form, though not in south-east Asian cookery. The fresh herb, lavishly added as a
garnish or salad leaf, is especially distinctive in Vietnamese dishes.

Mirin

A sweet Japanese rice wine for cooking.
Chinese Shaohsing is not really an accept-
able substitute.

Mooli radish

This giant white root vegetable, which
is sometimes called white winter radish,

is very similar to Japanese *daikon*.
Peel before using.

Oyster mushrooms

Oyster mushrooms have a distinctive
woody flavour. Although a commonly
occurring wild fungus, cultivated varieties
come in bright yellow, salmon pink, white
and dove grey varieties, and these are
often stocked in supermarkets.

Oyster sauce

An indispensable Chinese bottled sauce
made from real oysters that is widely used
in the cooking of southern China. It is not
fishy but has a subtle savoury flavour.

Pak choy

A delicious brassica that is also called
Chinese white cabbage, and resembles
Swiss chard in both appearance and taste.
Some varieties have a distinctive white
stem, others are pale green. Available in
Chinese supermarkets and some large
national supermarket branches.

Peanut oil

Also called groundnut oil, this is the
oil most used in Chinese cooking. It has
a mild flavour and can withstand great
heat before burning, making it ideal for
stir-frying.

Red onions

These lovely purplish onions are
commonly available. They are mild and

sweet and retain much of their colour when lightly cooked.

Rice vinegar

Rice vinegar varies in strength and colour from clear and pale yellow to red and even soy-coloured. When rice vinegar is specified in the recipes I suggest you use the clear or pale Japanese varieties, which are generally mellow and mild. Rice vinegar is available in Oriental supermarkets and some large, national supermarket branches.

Sake

This Japanese rice wine is clear and fragrant. Indispensable in Japanese cooking, *sake* is also a beverage. *Sake* may be quite difficult to obtain but Sainsbury's have recently introduced it in their largest branches.

Sesame oil

I generally use dark, Chinese sesame oil, which is the kind most suited to these recipes. This highly fragrant oil is best used as a flavouring as it burns easily. It is sold in small bottles because it quickly spoils. Available from Chinese supermarkets and some national supermarket branches.

Sesame seeds

These delicious, nutty seeds are best toasted and added as a garnish, or mixed into dipping sauces or Oriental salad dressings. Buy only in small quantities as they quickly go rancid. To toast, simply heat a small frying pan. Add the seeds when the pan is very hot and stir around until they begin to colour.

Shallots

There are many shallot varieties, ranging from the large, elongated yellow-skinned shallots to the more common rounded ones and the small, red-skinned Asian varieties. The flavour is mild but with a slight garlicky tone. Shallots make an excellent alternative to onions and are widely available, though the small red ones will only be obtained in Chinese supermarkets.

Shaohsing wine

One of the indispensable ingredients in Chinese cooking, this rice wine has a dark amber colour and a rich, sherry-like fragrance and flavour. Shaohsing wine is available in Chinese supermarkets. Some Safeway branches also stock it in their exotic foods section.

Shiitake mushrooms

This excellent fungus is available fresh and dried. Dried shiitake mushrooms must be soaked for at least half an hour in hot water, the tough stalks removed, and the caps thinly sliced. The delicious soaking liquid may be added to broths, soups and sauces. They are sometimes called 'Chinese mushrooms' and vary in colour from pale buff to dark brown or black.

Soba concentrate, noodle broth concentrate

This dark Japanese concentrate is usually available in clear plastic or glass bottles and may also be called 'concentrated soba sauce' or 'soup base for noodles'. Most brands contain soy sauce, dried bonito shavings, sugar, and *mirin* or *sake*. (See page 57 for details of diluting.) Only available in Japanese food shops or by mail order (see page 141).

Soy sauces

Perhaps the single most distinctive ingredient in Chinese, Korean, Japanese and other Oriental cuisines, soy sauce is an ancient savoury and salty liquid that has become very widely available. It is made from soy beans, flour and water, fermented, aged and distilled. Although there are several varieties, the principal Chinese soy sauces are 'light' and 'dark'. Kikkoman's is an excellent, complex Japanese brand that shares the characteristics of light and dark soy sauces.

Spring onions (scallions)

Together with ginger and garlic, spring onions, which are sometimes called salad onions, are an essential flavouring in Chinese cooking and other Oriental cuisines. They have a delicious mild flavour that is less intrusive than other members of the allium family. The white part and the green leaves may both be used, the latter generally as a raw garnish. Spring onions give a tangy, savoury flavour to many noodle dishes and are widely available throughout the year.

Squash: acorn, pattypan

These sweet-tasting squashes are most delicious when young and firm, and their flavour marries well with tomatoes, garlic and fresh herbs. They are occasionally available in supermarkets, but courgettes (zucchini), which belong to the same family, may be substituted.

Thai 7-spice seasoning

A zesty mixture of ground spices, including chilies, dried garlic, ginger, coriander seeds, lemon peel, cumin, and star anise.

Tiger prawns (shrimp)

These large south-east Asian shellfish are available raw from Chinese fishmongers, having previously been frozen, and the larger national supermarket branches also sell cooked tiger prawns. Other large prawns may be substituted but avoid the ubiquitous frozen Atlantic variety, which are tasteless and mushy.

Turmeric

An indispensable spice in Asian cookery, turmeric is actually a rhizome. Although sometimes found in its fresh form it is far more commonly available as a vivid

yellow powder. The flavour is warm
and subtle.

Wasabi

A root with a similar hot, fragrant
pungency to horseradish, although the
parent plant is unrelated to that familiar
European weed. *Wasabi*, which is native to
Japan was, until recently, only available
from Japanese food shops, either in
powdered form or as a pale green paste
rather like a tube of toothpaste. Now you
will find it in the larger branches of
Sainsbury's. Use sparingly.

Water chestnuts

A delicious aquatic vegetable produced by
a reed-like plant, water chestnuts are
commonly available canned. You may
also find fresh water chestnuts in Oriental
supermarkets. Do not overcook them.

Those recipes marked with the V symbol
are suitable for vegetarians.

NOODLE SOUPS AND WET NOODLE DISHES

There is nothing better for informal, cold-weather eating than a piping-hot bowl of steaming, delicately-scented, soupy noodles. In Japan, where these wet noodle dishes are especially popular, the 'done' thing is to slurp up the noodles without decorum. It is not considered rude to make so much noise when eating, and the slurping oxygenates the broth, which makes it tastier.

The following recipes borrow widely from Oriental cuisines. Many, such as *Zesty Thai noodle soup, Korean beef and noodle soup, 'Street' noodles*, and most of the Japanese recipes, are adapted from authentic recipes. Some – *Noodle soup with curried chicken and aubergine in coconut milk*, and *Vietnamese-style chicken noodle soup* – are entirely my own creation but are rooted, nonetheless, in Oriental cookery. A few others, such as *Hot and fragrant noodle soup with prawns and lemon grass* are adapted from traditional dishes but are transformed by the unorthodox addition of noodles. Other recipes deliberately mix eastern and western ingredients to great effect. Try, for example, *Noodles in spicy tomato sauce with fried bean curd*, and *Noodles in broth with mussels, lemon grass and coriander*...you won't be disappointed by the exciting marriage of flavours.

Good quality stock (broth) is fundamental to successful cookery, but nowhere is this more vital than in soupy dishes. You may find my basic recipes for chicken, beef and vegetable stock useful, and the *dashi* recipe is deliciously delicate.

If serving in individual portions you will need very large soup bowls. For that reason I prefer to serve most of these wet dishes from a soup tureen or a large, steep-sided bowl. Be sure to divide the noodles in equal measures, and pour a generous volume of broth over them.

v Vegetarian Noodle Soup

Although substantial, full-flavoured and delicious, this noodle soup contains no meat or fish, and makes the perfect healthy light lunch or supper for four people.

12 dried shiitake mushrooms
100g/4oz thin, dried egg noodles
2 tbsp peanut oil
1 large carrot, scrubbed and finely diced
1 stick (stalk) of celery, finely diced
50g/2oz button mushrooms, thinly sliced
100g/4oz canned water chestnuts, drained
    and thinly sliced
2 fresh, ripe but fairly firm tomatoes,
    peeled and diced
4 Chinese cabbage leaves, shredded
2 tbsp Shaohsing wine
1.2 litres/2 pints/5 cups vegetable
    stock/broth (see page 51)
100g/4oz solid bean curd, cut into
    2cm/3/4 inch cubes
2 tbsp light soy sauce
1 tbsp dark soy sauce
2 tbsp rice vinegar
2 tsp sugar
salt and freshly ground black pepper
white part of 4 spring onions (scallions),
    finely chopped
2 tsp flour mixed with 3 tbsp water
small handful of fresh coriander (cilantro),
    chopped

Soak the shiitake mushrooms in a cup of hot water for 30 minutes to reconstitute them. Strain and reserve the water. Slice the shiitake caps very thinly, discarding the tough stalks. Boil the egg noodles in abundant water until al dente, stirring to separate the strands, then rinse, drain and put into a soup tureen or a large serving bowl with steep sides.

Heat 1 tbsp oil to smoking point in a wok. Add the carrots, celery, the shiitake and button mushrooms and the water chestnuts; stir-fry for 1 minute. Add the tomatoes, cabbage leaves and the Shaohsing wine, cook for 30 seconds, then set aside off the heat while you bring to the boil in another large pan the stock together with the shiitake mushrooms' soaking liquid.

In a small frying pan heat 1 tbsp oil to smoking point, add the bean curd, then reduce the heat slightly and fry on all sides until pale golden. Lift and drain on absorbent paper.

Add the wok contents to the stock pan, then add the soy sauces, vinegar, sugar, seasoning, and spring onions. Return to the boil, reduce the heat, and simmer for 4–5 minutes, then add the flour dissolved in water, stir, and allow the soup to thicken a little. Add the bean curd and coriander, mix, bring back to a simmer, then pour over the noodles and serve straight away.

Rice 'Vermicelli' Soup

A delicious and nourishing Chinese-style noodle soup, best made with a rich, home-made stock. Serves two to three people.

1 tsp corn flour
1 tbsp water
1¹/₂ tbsp Shaohsing wine
1¹/₂ tbsp light soy sauce
salt and freshly ground black pepper
175g/6oz skinned chicken breast,
*   cut into small, thin strips*
100g/4oz canned, sliced bamboo shoots,
*   rinsed and drained*
bunch of watercress, lower stalks
*   trimmed off*
100g/4oz thin rice noodles ('vermicelli')
1 litre/1³/₄ pints/4 ¹/₃ cups chicken
*   stock/broth (see page 50)*
3 tbsp peanut oil
2 spring onions (scallions), finely chopped
1 fresh chili, seeded and finely chopped
1 tbsp dark soy sauce
¹/₂ tsp sugar
2 tsp sesame oil

Mix the corn flour, water, and 2 tsp each of Shaohsing wine and light soy sauce. Season generously with salt and pepper, add the chicken strips and combine thoroughly. Slice the bamboo shoots into thin strips. Coarsely chop the watercress.

Bring a large pan of water to the boil, add the 'vermicelli' and cook briefly until nearly *al dente*. Rinse under cold water and drain. Bring the stock to the boil in a pan, then turn off the heat. Add the 'vermi-celli' to the pan containing the stock, cover and set aside.

With a slotted spoon, remove the chicken from the marinade, saving the liquid. Heat the oil to smoking point in a wok. Put in the chicken and stir-fry for 1 minute, then add all the vegetables, including the spring onions and chili, and stir-fry for 1 minute longer. Add the marinade liquid, the remaining light soy sauce and Shaohsing wine, the dark soy sauce and the sugar. Mix well, then add the wok contents to the pan containing the stock and noodles. Return to the boil, sprinkle with the sesame oil, and serve immediately.

Zesty Thai Noodle Soup

In this quick and easy dish the cooked and raw ingredients are piled on top of each other, and the hot stock is added when you are ready to eat. Serves two to three people.

100g/4oz thin, dried egg noodles
100g/4oz bean sprouts
75g/3oz cooked ham, cut into matchstick strips
75g/3oz cooked, peeled prawns (shrimp), thawed if frozen
1 'little gem' lettuce, shredded
2 spring onions (scallions), thinly sliced
leaves from 3 sprigs of basil, chopped
leaves from 3 sprigs of mint, chopped
2 tsp peanut oil
5 cloves of garlic, peeled and thinly sliced
1 litre/1³/4 pints/4¹/3 cups chicken stock/broth (see page 50)
1 tbsp fish sauce
1 tbsp light soy sauce
juice of 1 lime
2 tsp sugar
50g/2oz roasted peanuts, lightly crushed
¹/2–1 tsp chili flakes (optional)

Bring a large pan of water to the boil, add the noodles, return to the boil and cook until just *al dente*, then rinse under cold water and drain. Put the noodles into a soup tureen or a large steep-sided bowl. Add the bean sprouts, ham, prawns, lettuce, spring onions and herbs.

Heat the oil in a small, non-stick frying pan, add the garlic and fry briefly until golden. Pour the pan contents into the tureen with the noodles and other ingredients.

Bring the stock to the boil, add the fish and soy sauces, the lime juice and sugar. Pour the stock over the noodles, sprinkle the peanuts and chili flakes on top and eat immediately.

Hot and Fragrant Noodle Soup with Prawns and Lemon Grass

This is a wonderful adaptation – with the addition of noodles – of the famous Thai soup *Tom yam gung*. For good results it is vital to obtain raw, unpeeled prawns: they will be juicier and more tender than cooked ones, and their shells are essential to the delicious flavour of the broth base. If using cooked prawns, make the stock without any shells and add the prawns to the pan right at the end. This soup is really quite fiery, but just omit the chili oil for a milder version. Serves two to three people, more if served as a starter.

50g/2oz thin rice noodles ('vermicelli')
225g/8oz raw, unshelled prawns (shrimp)
2 kaffir lime leaves, sliced
tender part of 2 sticks (stalks) of lemon
  grass, chopped
1.2 litres/2 pints/5 cups chicken stock/broth
  (see page 50)
juice of 2 limes
1 tbsp light soy sauce
1 tbsp fish sauce
6 fresh button mushrooms, very thinly
  sliced
1 fresh chili, seeded and very thinly sliced
2 spring onions (scallions), very thinly
sliced
1–3 tsp chili oil (optional)
leaves from 8 sprigs of fresh coriander
  (cilantro), chopped

Snap the 'vermicelli' into small strands: do this in a paper bag to contain the shards. Bring a large pan of water to the boil, add the 'vermicelli' and turn off the heat. When almost *al dente* remove, rinse and drain. Put the 'vermicelli' in the bottom of a soup tureen or large serving bowl with steep sides.

Wash and peel the prawns. Put the shells into a large pan, together with the lime leaves, lemon grass, chicken stock, and lime juice. Bring the broth to the boil, reduce the heat, cover and simmer for 15 minutes to extract flavour. Strain into a pan and add the prawns. Pour in the soy and fish sauces, add the mushrooms, chili and spring onions. Heat without boiling, cover the pan and simmer for 2–3 minutes. If desired, add the chili oil. (Add cooked prawns now, if appropriate, and rest with the lid on for 1 minute.) Add the coriander, then pour the pan contents over the noodles and serve straight away.

Hot and Sour Noodle Soup

This is an adaptation of a popular Chinese soup. I have increased the proportion of noodles to liquid to make a nourishing and more substantial dish for four people.

40g/1¹/₂oz dried shiitake mushrooms
75g/3oz thin rice noodles ('vermicelli')
2 tsp peanut oil
75g/3oz ham, diced
1.25 litres/2¹/₄ pints/5¹/₂ cups chicken
   stock/broth (see page 50)
75g/3oz oyster mushrooms, diced
100g/4oz solid bean curd, finely diced
2 tbsp light soy sauce
1 tbsp dark soy sauce
4 tbsp rice vinegar
2 tbsp Shaohsing wine
2 tsp sugar
salt and freshly ground black pepper
4 spring onions (scallions), thinly sliced
1 tbsp flour mixed with 2 tbsp water
2 eggs, beaten
1 tbsp sesame oil
2 tsp chili oil (or to taste)
handful of fresh coriander (cilantro),
   chopped

Soak the shiitake mushrooms in a cup of hot water for 30 minutes to reconstitute them. Strain and reserve the water. Slice the shiitake caps very thinly, discarding the tough stalks. Soak the noodles in water as recommended on the packet. When soft, drain and reserve them.

Fry the ham in a small pan until golden. Bring the stock and the mushrooms' soaking liquid to a boil in a large pot. Add the ham, the reconstituted and fresh mushrooms, the noodles, bean curd, soy sauces, vinegar, Shaohsing wine, sugar, seasoning, and the spring onions. Return to the boil, reduce the heat, and simmer for 3–4 minutes, then add the flour dissolved in water, stir, and allow the soup to thicken a little. Stir in the beaten eggs in a very thin stream and pull in different directions with a fork, to stretch the eggs as they set. Add the sesame and chili oils, mix, and simmer for a minute longer. Sprinkle with the coriander and eat straight away.

Thai Noodle Soup

This excellent dish, which in reality is too substantial to qualify as a soup, provides a delicious, nourishing meal for four people. The noodles and prawns may be eaten first, then the liquid remaining can be slurped up like soup. Raw prawns give the best flavour, but very large species such as tiger prawns should be chopped into 2cm/¾ inch pieces. Cooked frozen prawns may be substituted successfully.

1 tbsp peanut oil
4 cloves of garlic, peeled and thinly sliced
100g/4oz cooked ham, finely diced
100g/4oz dried egg noodles
100g/4oz fresh bean sprouts
1.5 litres/2½ pints/6¼ cups chicken
   stock/broth (see page 50)
2 sticks (stalks) of lemon grass, bruised and
   thinly sliced
2 fresh or dried kaffir lime leaves, thinly
   sliced (optional)
75g/3oz raw or cooked prawns/shrimp
(properly thawed if bought frozen), peeled
100g/4oz Chinese leaf cabbage, shredded
100g/4oz button mushrooms, very thinly
   sliced
2 tsp sugar
1 tbsp Thai fish sauce
1 tbsp light soy sauce
1 tbsp Shaohsing wine
2 tbsp roasted peanuts, crushed
½–1 tsp chili flakes (or to taste)
4 spring onions (scallions), thinly sliced
small handful of fresh coriander (cilantro),
   chopped

Heat the oil in a small non-stick pan. Stir-fry the garlic and ham over a moderate heat until pale golden, taking care not to burn them. Remove to a plate lined with absorbent paper. Boil the noodles until tender or as directed by the packet instructions. Rinse under cold water and drain well. Put them into a soup tureen or a steep-sided serving bowl. Add the bean sprouts, garlic and ham and mix together.

Bring the stock to the boil, together with the lemon grass and lime leaves. Add the raw prawns (cooked prawns should not be added until the end of the cooking), cabbage, mushrooms, sugar, fish and soy sauces, and the Shaohsing wine. Cover and simmer for 3 minutes. Add the cooked prawns (if using) and pour the pan contents over the noodles, stir to mix, then sprinkle the peanuts, chilies, spring onions and coriander over the soup. Serve straight away.

Vietnamese-style Chicken Noodle Soup

Hot, salty and sour, minty and redolent of fresh coriander, this is a wonderful noodle dish. The soup itself is relatively bland, but the little bowls of chili garnishes – one mixed with lime juice and fish sauce, the other with rice vinegar and soy sauce – determine much of the flavour and pungency. Add to the soup as much of each garnish as you think you can handle, but be cautious initially! Serves two to three people.

1 clove of garlic, peeled and crushed
2 tbsp fish sauce
juice of 2 limes
5 tsp sugar
1/2 tsp cayenne
6 fresh chilies, seeded and finely chopped
3 tbsp rice vinegar
1 tbsp light soy sauce
50g/2oz roasted peanuts, lightly crushed
100g/4oz dried, ribbon rice noodles
1 litre/1 3/4 pints/4 1/3 cups chicken
stock/broth (see page 50)
175g/6oz skinless, boned chicken, cut into
very small, thin strips
2 spring onions (scallions), trimmed and
finely chopped
leaves from 6 sprigs of coriander (cilantro),
chopped
leaves from 6 sprigs of mint, chopped

Combine in a small bowl the garlic, fish sauce, lime juice, 3 tsp sugar and the cayenne. Mix well and set aside. In a second bowl combine half the chopped chilies with the vinegar and light soy sauce. Put the crushed peanuts into another little bowl.

Bring a large pan of water to the boil, add the rice noodles and cook until *al dente*. Rinse under cold water and drain. Bring the stock to the boil, add the chicken, return to the boil, then reduce the heat and simmer until the chicken is cooked – about 5 minutes.

Add the noodles to the hot stock and leave for 1 minute. Remove the noodles and chicken with a slotted spoon or strainer and divide between two or three large soup bowls. Cover with equal portions of spring onions and herbs, and sprinkle with the remaining chopped chilies and 2 tsp sugar. Return the stock to the boil, then pour it over the noodles. Serve immediately. Add the nuts and chili garnishes to taste.

Noodle Soup with Curried Chicken and Aubergine in Coconut Milk

This headily fragrant, wonderfully flavourful soup is really a liquid curry cooked with Thai ingredients. It is quick and easy to make without sacrificing authenticity. Absolutely delicious on its own for a light lunch or supper, this serves two to three people.

75g/3oz thin rice noodles ('vermicelli')
1 chicken breast, skinned and cut into
    2cm/3/4 inch chunks
1 small, firm aubergine (eggplant), trimmed
    and cut into 2cm/3/4 inch chunks
2 shallots, peeled and sliced
2 cloves of garlic, peeled and finely
    chopped
2 lime leaves, thinly sliced
grated rind and juice of 1/2 lemon
1 tbsp fish sauce
1 tbsp light soy sauce
1 tsp salt
1 tsp sugar
1 tbsp Thai 'red' curry paste
250ml/8fl oz/1 cup canned coconut milk
1-2 fresh chilies, seeded and thinly sliced
600ml/1 pint/2 1/2 cups chicken stock/broth
    (see page 50)
leaves from 2 sprigs of basil

Snap the 'vermicelli' into small strands, preferably in a paper bag to contain the shards. Bring a large pan of water to the boil, add the 'vermicelli' and turn off the heat. When, after a few minutes, they are nearly *al dente*, remove, rinse under cold water and drain.

Put into a medium-sized lidded pan the chicken, aubergine, shallots, garlic, lime leaf strips, lemon rind and juice, fish and soy sauces, salt, sugar, curry paste and coconut milk. Mix, cover, bring to the boil, then reduce the heat and simmer for 20 minutes or until the chicken and aubergine are tender. Add the chilies, chicken stock and the noodles, return to a simmer and cook for 1–2 minutes longer. Add the basil and serve from the pan or transfer into a soup tureen or steep-sided bowl.

Korean Chicken Noodle Soup

The amount of cayenne added determines the heat in this fiery but delicious Korean soup so adjust to suit your own tolerance level! This makes enough for four to six people.

2.25 litres/4 pints/10 cups chicken
  stock/broth (see page 50)
225g/8oz skinless chicken meat (trimmed
  weight)
1 large carrot, scrubbed
2 tsp–1 tbsp cayenne, according to taste
3 tbsp light soy sauce plus a little extra to
  season
1 tbsp sesame oil
1 tbsp sesame seeds, lightly toasted in a hot,
  dry frying pan
freshly ground black pepper, to taste
225g/8oz thin, dried wheat noodles such as
  Japanese somen
3 tbsp water
1 tsp salt
4cm/1¹/₂ inch piece of fresh ginger, peeled
4 cloves of garlic, peeled
white part of 6 spring onions (scallions)
1 tbsp rice vinegar

Bring the stock to boil, add the chicken, return to a simmer, cover, and cook for about 10–12 minutes or until tender. Add the whole carrot halfway through the simmering. Remove the chicken and carrot and reserve the stock. Shred the chicken as finely as possible and finely dice the carrot. Put the shredded chicken and diced carrot in a bowl, add the cayenne, 3 tbsp soy sauce and the sesame oil. Add the toasted sesame seeds and a grinding of black pepper and mix thoroughly. Set aside.

Return the stock to the boil, add the noodles and cook until almost *al dente*. Meanwhile grind to a paste in a food processor the water, salt, ginger, garlic and spring onions. Add the paste to the pot containing the noodles and stock, and mix well. Return to the boil, and when the noodles are *al dente*, add the chicken mixture, the vinegar and additional soy sauce, to taste. Eat straight away, either served from the pot or from a soup tureen.

Korean Beef and Noodle Soup

An easy, delicious soup that is a meal in itself. Thin Japanese *somen* noodles work well but other noodles may be substituted. The dash of chili oil gives a much needed pungency to what otherwise would be a slightly bland dish. Serves two to three people.

1 tbsp corn oil
1 egg plus 1 egg yolk, beaten
100g/4oz dried somen noodles
100g/4oz beef sirloin or rump steak,
    (trimmed weight)
1 red onion, peeled
small handful of chives
75g/3oz bean sprouts
50g/2oz pak choy or Chinese leaf cabbage
1.2 litres/2 pints/5 cups beef or vegetable
    stock/broth (see page 49 or 51)
salt and freshly ground black pepper
1/2 tsp sugar
2 tbsp light soy sauce
2 spring onions (scallions)
1/4–1 tsp chili oil

Heat 2 tsp of the oil in a wok. When smoking pour in the beaten egg and make an omelette. Drain on absorbent paper, and slice into neat, thin strips.

Bring a large pan of water to the boil, add the noodles and cook until nearly *al dente* (very briefly if *somen* noodles are used). Rinse under cold water and drain. Meanwhile cut the beef into small, thin strips. Halve the onion from top to bottom and slice thinly. Snip the chives. Thinly slice the spring onions. Halve the bean sprouts. Shred and dice the *pak choy* or Chinese leaf cabbage.

Heat the remaining oil in a wok. When smoking add the beef, stir-fry for 1 1/2 minutes, then add all the vegetables except for the spring onions. Stir-fry for 1 minute longer and reserve. Bring the stock to the boil in a pan, add the vegetables and the beef and simmer for 2 minutes. Add the noodles, season with salt, pepper and sugar, add the soy sauce, then transfer to a soup tureen or serve from the pan. Sprinkle with the spring onions, add the omelette strips and a few drops of chili oil. Eat while still piping hot.

'Street' Noodles

This is my version of the delicious soupy lunch-time noodles dispensed by street vendors in south-east Asia. For the optimum noodle size and texture I prefer fresh, white, wheat ribbon noodles such as Japanese *kishimen*. In Thailand, where this is a very popular snack, fresh rice noodles would be used, but in fact any noodles may be substituted. A truly excellent dish, and enough for three people.

450g/1lb fresh egg ribbon noodles
600ml/1 pint/2½ cups chicken
  stock/broth (see page 50)
2 tbsp peanut oil
1 red onion, peeled, halved from top to
  bottom and thinly sliced
2 cloves of garlic, peeled and thinly sliced
2 tsp Thai 'red' curry paste
150ml/5fl oz/⅔ cup gado-gado peanut
  sauce (see page 68)
1 tbsp fish sauce
juice of 1 lime
1 tsp sugar
75g/3oz bean sprouts
100g/4oz cooked, skinless chicken,
  shredded
75g/3oz peeled, cooked jumbo or tiger
  prawns (shrimp), thawed if frozen
small handful of fresh coriander (cilantro),
  chopped
½–1 tsp chili flakes (optional)
pinch of Thai '7-spice seasoning' (optional)

Bring abundant water to the boil, add the fresh noodles, return to the boil and cook briefly until just *al dente*. (Follow the packet instructions for dried noodles, and as a rough rule of thumb reckon on about half the weight specified for fresh ones.) Rinse the noodles under cold water and drain. In another pan, bring the stock to the boil, then cover and set aside. Put the noodles into a large steep-sided bowl or soup tureen.

Heat the oil to smoking point in a wok. Add the onion and garlic, toss for 2 minutes, then add the curry paste, peanut sauce, fish sauce, lime juice, and sugar. Stir for a few seconds to release aromas, then add the bean sprouts, turn a few times and add the cooked chicken and prawns. Pour in the stock, bring to the boil and pour over the noodles. Scatter with coriander and, if desired, the chili flakes and seasoning. Eat immediately.

Alternative garnishes:
Add or substitute several or any of the following: thin strips of omelette; thinly sliced spring onions (scallions), fresh chilies, or cucumber; quartered limes; shredded lettuce heart; crisply fried shallots; crisp bacon bits.

v Noodles in Spicy Tomato Sauce with Fried Bean Curd

This is a spicier, Oriental version of spaghetti in tomato sauce, and is another example of how classic pasta dishes can be re-invented with a base of noodles and the zesty ingredients typical of south-east Asian cooking. Serves three to four people.

225g/8oz dried egg noodles
400g/14oz premium quality canned plum
    tomatoes, chopped
4 tbsp peanut oil
3 cloves of garlic, peeled and finely
    chopped
2cm/3/4 inch piece of fresh ginger, peeled
    and finely chopped
1 kaffir lime leaf, thinly sliced
2–3 fresh chilies, seeded and finely
chopped
1 tbsp light soy sauce
1 tsp sugar
100g/4oz solid bean curd, cut into
    1cm/1/2 inch cubes
generous handful of fresh coriander
    (cilantro), chopped

Bring abundant water to the boil, add the noodles and boil until al dente, then rinse under cold water and drain.

Put the tomatoes, 2 tbsp oil and all the other ingredients down to the sugar in a large pan. Bring to the boil, then reduce the heat and simmer for 15–20 minutes or until thick. Set aside. Heat the remaining 2 tbsp oil in a non-stick frying pan, add the bean curd and fry until golden all over. Tip the noodles into the pan with the tomato sauce and re-heat thoroughly, turning the noodles in the sauce. Transfer the pan contents into a warmed serving bowl, sprinkle the coriander on top and scatter over the fried bean curd. Eat straight away.

[v] Noodles with Braised Broccoli, Water Chestnuts and Bean Curd

Although by no means soupy, this is quite a moist noodle dish which may be eaten on its own as a substantial snack or as a healthy light meal. The soft, braised bean curd contrasts very pleasantly with the crunchy water chestnuts and peanut garnish. Although entirely meatless, there is plenty of protein in this delicious recipe, but strict vegetarians may omit the oyster sauce. Serves two to three people.

225g/8oz broccoli
100g/4oz thin, dried egg noodles
2 tbsp peanut oil
6 small red or 3 yellow shallots, peeled and
    sliced
3 cloves of garlic, peeled and thinly sliced
175g/6oz canned water chestnuts, drained
    and coarsely chopped
225g/8oz solid bean curd, cut into
    2cm/3/4 inch dice
1 tbsp Shaohsing wine
2 tbsp oyster sauce
1 tbsp light soy sauce
120ml/4fl oz/1/2 cup vegetable stock/broth
    (see page 51) or water
50g/2oz roasted peanuts, crushed
small handful of fresh coriander (cilantro),
    chopped
1–2 tbsp Kikkoman's soy sauce or to taste

Divide the broccoli into small florets and bite-sized chunks, including the upper part of the stem. Bring plenty of salted water to the boil. Add the broccoli, return to the boil and cook for 2 minutes. Saving the water, remove the broccoli with a slotted spoon, plunge into cold water and drain. Return the water to the boil, add the noodles, stir to separate the strands, and cook until *al dente*. Rinse under cold water and drain.

Heat the oil to smoking point in a wok, add the shallots and garlic and stir-fry for 30 seconds. Add the broccoli and water chestnuts and stir-fry for 2 minutes longer, then add the bean curd, Shaohsing wine, the oyster and light soy sauces, and the stock or water. Bring to the boil, then cover the wok, reduce the heat and simmer for 2 minutes longer or until the broccoli is tender. Add the noodles, raise the heat and toss until they have heated through. Transfer the wok contents to a serving dish, scatter the peanuts and coriander on top. Season, if desired, with the additional soy sauce. and eat immediately.

v Deep-fried Rice 'Vermicelli' with Braised Vegetables

The whole point of this very pretty dish –
a splendid vegetarian variation on the
festive Thai dish *Mee krob* (see page 104)–
is the contrast between the crisp rice
noodles and colourful *al dente* vegetables
bathed in a rich spicy sauce. Do not be put
off if, after a while, the crisp noodle base
is made pulpy by the sauce, but do eat as
soon as possible after the dish is complet-
ed. Your guests should serve themselves
small individual portions, so should be
served alongside several other Oriental
dishes, and some plain boiled rice. That
way, it will serve at least six people.

peanut or corn oil for deep frying plus 3 tbsp
175g/6oz thin rice noodles ('vermicelli')
3 cloves of garlic, peeled and thinly sliced
2cm/3/4 inch piece of fresh ginger, peeled
*   and finely chopped*
75g/3oz baby corn
1 red pepper, seeded, de-pithed and
*   coarsely chopped*
1 green pepper, seeded, de-pithed and
*   coarsely chopped*
3 firm baby aubergines (eggplant), cut
*   into 2cm/3/4 inch cubes*
3 ripe fresh tomatoes, peeled and chopped
1 tbsp Shaohsing wine
1 tsp sugar
1/2 tsp salt
2 tbsp yellow bean sauce
2 tsp chili sauce
2 tbsp light soy sauce
2 tsp rice vinegar
120ml/4fl oz/ 1/2 cup vegetable
*   stock/broth (see page 51)*

4 spring onions (scallions), trimmed
and sliced, the white and green parts
*   separated*
75g/3oz bean sprouts
50g/2oz cashews, coarsely chopped

Heat a deep layer of oil in a wok until
quite a lot of smoke rises. Meanwhile, put
the noodles in a bag and pull them apart
into clumps. Test a few strands before deep-
frying the clumps: if they immediately
crackle and swell, the oil has reached the
right temperature. Add the noodle clumps
to the wok in batches, and fry until well
puffed and a light golden colour, turning
each batch once, then remove with a large
wire strainer or slotted spoon and drain on
absorbent paper .

   When all the clumps have been deep-
fried, place them on a very large serving
dish and keep them warm in a cool oven
while you make the sauce.

   Clean the wok and heat 3 tbsp oil to
smoking point. Add the garlic and ginger,
stir for a few seconds, then add the corn,
peppers, aubergines and tomatoes. Stir-fry
for about 2 minutes, then add the
Shaohsing wine, sugar, salt, the bean and
chili sauces, light soy sauce, vinegar and
stock. Cook for 1–2 minutes longer or until
the vegetables are just *al dente*, then add
the white part of the spring onions and the
bean sprouts and cook for 30 seconds
longer. Pour the vegetables and their sauce
over the noodles, sprinkle with the
cashews and the green part of the spring
onions, and serve immediately.

Noodles with Beef and Broccoli in Oyster Sauce

A mild but pleasantly flavoured, wet noodle dish with Thai origins. It is quite substantial and serves three to four people.

200g/7oz broccoli
200g/7oz piece of beef rump or sirloin
*   steak, trimmed*
1 tsp flour
2 tbsp water
2 tbsp peanut or corn oil
1 small red onion, peeled and thinly sliced
3 cloves of garlic, peeled and thinly sliced
350ml/12fl oz/1½ cups beef stock/broth
*   (see page 49)*
2 tbsp oyster sauce
1 tbsp light soy sauce
1 tsp sugar
salt and freshly ground black pepper
450g/1lb fresh 'oil' noodles (preferably the
*   white, egg-less variety)*

Trim off the bottom end of the broccoli stalks and slice the stems and florets at a diagonal angle into 1cm/½ inch sections. Cut the beef into small, thin strips. Put the broccoli into a small pan, add enough lightly salted water to cover, bring to the boil and cook until nearly tender. Refresh under cold water and drain. Dissolve the flour in 2 tbsp water and set aside.

Heat the oil to smoking point in a wok, add the beef, onion and garlic and stir-fry for 3–4 minutes, then add the cooked broccoli, the flour mixture, beef stock, the oyster and soy sauces, sugar, and season. Return to the boil, add the noodles and simmer for 2–3 minutes longer. Serve very hot.

Udon Noodles with Char-grilled Beef, Green Pepper and Black Beans

A well-flavoured dish of fat *udon* noodles in black bean sauce. Serves two people.

450g/1lb fresh or 225g/8oz dried udon
   noodles
1 tbsp sesame oil
175g/6oz rump or sirloin steak, trimmed
freshly ground black pepper
2 tbsp Kikkoman's soy sauce or dark soy
   sauce
2 tbsp mirin
1 tbsp sake
1/2 tsp flour
6 tbsp beef stock/broth (see page 49) or
   water
2 tbsp peanut oil
2 cloves of garlic, peeled and thinly sliced
1 cm/1/2 inch piece of fresh ginger, peeled
   and finely chopped
1 small green pepper, seeded, de-pithed
   and diced
2 tbsp fermented black beans, rinsed,
   drained and chopped

Bring a large pan of water to the boil, add the noodles, return to the boil and cook until nearly *al dente*: (15–30 seconds for fresh noodles, follow the packet instructions for dried). Rinse under cold water and drain. Toss the noodles in sesame oil and set aside. Slice the steak into small, thin strips, put them in a bowl and season with pepper. Mix together the soy sauce, 1 tbsp *mirin*, and the *sake*. Pour over the beef, mix to coat and set aside for 30 minutes. Dissolve the flour in the stock or water.

Heat a cast-iron griddle or a heavy cast-iron frying pan. When very hot, lift the beef from the marinade, saving the latter, and drain. Sear it for about 45 seconds on each side, then remove and reserve. Heat the peanut oil to smoking point in a wok, add the garlic and ginger, stir a few times, then add the green pepper. Stir-fry for 30 seconds, then add the black beans and stir-fry for 30 seconds longer. Pour in the remaining 1 tbsp *mirin*, the marinade and the stock or water. Bring to the boil, add the noodles and beef and toss to coat in the black bean sauce. When the noodles have heated through, divide them between two large soup bowls or deep plates and eat immediately.

Udon Noodles in Broth

This is one of the simplest of soupy Japanese noodle dishes. *Shichimi* (Japanese 7-spice mixture) is the traditional seasoning for *udon* noodles in broth. It comprises flaked red peppers, ground *sansho* pods, flaked mandarin orange peel, hemp and poppy seeds, *nori* seaweed, and sesame seeds. It is quite elusive but is sometimes stocked in Japanese shops. You can substitute Chinese '5-spice powder' or even Thai '7-spice seasoning' for an altogether different flavour. If you want a pungent underlying heat stir in a little *wasabi* or horseradish. This recipe makes four to six servings.

450g/1lb dried udon noodles
1 litre/1 ³/4 pints/4 ¹/3 cups Japanese
    noodle broth (see page 53)
6 spring onions (scallions), finely chopped
generous pinch shichimi (see above) or to
    taste
2–3 tsp wasabi or prepared horseradish
    (optional)
4–6 tbsp Kikkoman's soy sauce (optional)

Bring a large pan of water to the boil, add the noodles, return to the boil and cook until *al dente*. Rinse under cold water, drain and put into a large, steep-sided bowl or soup tureen. Bring the noodle broth to the boil in a large pan, pour it over the noodles, scatter the spring onions, and sprinkle the spice mixture on top. Add the *wasabi* or horseradish, and soy sauce, if desired, and eat immediately.

Soba Noodles in Broth

Another quick Japanese dish, this time with delicious, nutty sesame seeds. The flavour depends upon the quality of the noodle broth. Bottled concentrate is certainly fast and convenient, but the fresh home-made version tastes best of all. Serves two to three people.

225g/8oz dried soba noodles

2 tsp sesame seeds

1.2 litres/2 pints/5 cups Japanese noodle broth (see page 53)

2cm/3/4 inch piece of fresh ginger, peeled and finely chopped

2 spring onions (scallions), trimmed and thinly sliced

1 fresh chili, seeded and finely chopped (optional)

Bring a large pan of water to the boil, add the noodles, return to the boil and cook until *al dente*, then rinse and drain. While the noodles boil, toast the sesame seeds in a hot, dry pan until they start to colour, remove from the pan and reserve. Put the noodles into a soup tureen or a large, steep-sided bowl. Bring the noodle broth to the boil and pour over the noodles. Scatter the ginger, spring onions, toasted sesame seeds and, if desired, the chili on top, and eat straight away.

Soba Noodles in Refreshing, Chilled Broth

A colourful and healthy salad which is wonderfully refreshing and makes an excellent light summer's lunch, serving two to three people.

4 tbsp soba concentrate/noodle broth
   concentrate
175ml/6fl oz/¾ cup dashi (see page 52)
   or chicken stock/broth (see page 50)
1 tbsp mirin
225g/8oz dried soba noodles
salt
75g/3oz thin, green beans, trimmed and
   cut into 2.5cm/1 inch sections
75g/3oz carrot, scrubbed, halved from end
   to end, and thinly sliced
75g/3oz baby corn, halved
1 small ridge cucumber or a 13cm/5 inch
   section, peeled
6 red radishes, quartered
6 cherry tomatoes, quartered
white part of 2 spring onions (scallions),
   trimmed and thinly sliced
salt and freshly ground pepper
3 tsp wasabi or to taste

Put into a small pan the concentrate, *dashi* or stock, and the *mirin*. Bring to a simmer and cook for 1 minute, allow to cool, then chill in the fridge.

Bring a large pan of water to the boil, add the noodles, return to the boil and cook until *al dente*. Save the water to blanch the vegetables. Rinse the noodles under cold water and drain.

When nearly ready to eat, check that the noodles have not stuck together. To remedy, give them a quick rinse, and drain. Divide the noodles into two or three serving portions and place in soup bowls. Re-heat the water to boiling point, add a little salt, and put in the beans, carrots and baby corn, return to a vigorous boil and cook for just 2 minutes. Rinse under cold water and drain. Halve the cucumber from end to end, scoop out the seedy middle with a teaspoon, and slice thinly. Garnish the noodles with all the vegetables, season lightly, pour over equal measures of the chilled broth, and top with small dollops of *wasabi*. Serve cold.

Variations:

The above ingredients are merely suggestions, and other blanched and raw vegetables may be substituted or added: chunks of lightly boiled asparagus; mangetouts (snow peas), shredded Chinese leaf cabbage or *pak choy*; Cos (romaine) lettuce; thin green pepper rings; diced sweet red or yellow pepper; thinly sliced mild white onion; *daikon* or mooli radish, to list but a few.

Soba Noodles with Tempura Prawns

This recipe is a very popular noodle combination in Japan. *Soba* (buckwheat) noodles and the broth concentrate will only be found in Japanese shops and in some Oriental supermarkets, and as the dish is so uncomplicated prime ingredients are essential. The tempura batter keeps the prawns deliciously succulent, and this is one recipe for which you will need large, whole raw prawns such as tiger prawns: cooked frozen prawns just will not do! The batter requires chilled water, which should be refrigerated several hours in advance. Serves three people.

225g/8oz dried soba noodles
100ml/4fl oz/^{1}/$_2$ cup soba concentrate/
*   noodle broth concentrate*
2 tsp sugar
1 litre/1^3/$_4$ pints/4^1/$_3$ cups dashi
(see page 52) or chicken stock/broth
*   (see page 50)*
1 tbsp mirin
225g/8oz large raw prawns/shrimp
*   (about 6)*
1 tsp salt
175g/6oz/1 heaped cup plain (all-purpose)
*   flour*
175ml/6fl oz/^{3}/$_4$ cup chilled water
2 tbsp rice vinegar
1 egg, beaten
sunflower oil for deep-frying
2 tsp sesame oil

Bring a large pan of water to the boil, add the *soba* noodles and cook until almost *al dente*; they will finish cooking in the hot broth. Rinse under cold water and drain.

Put into a small pan the concentrate, sugar, the *dashi* or stock, and the *mirin*. Peel and wash the prawns, but leave the fanned tips of the tail sections unpeeled; sprinkle the prawns with half of the salt and set aside.

Prepare the batter: put the flour into a bowl, make a well, and sprinkle with the remaining salt; pour in the refrigerated water, the vinegar and the egg, then whisk vigorously, folding in the flour from the sides. Continue until the batter is smooth and creamy: neither watery nor thick and sticky, it should fall off the whisk in discernible heavy drips. Keep refrigerated until the dipping stage.

Re-heat the broth to simmering point, add the noodles, cover and set aside, off the heat. Heat a deep layer of oil in a wok. As soon as the oil starts to smoke, test a drip of batter: if it sinks to the bottom it is not yet hot enough. Test another drip a little later: when it instantly fizzles and crackles submerge the prawns in the batter one by one, holding them by their tails, then carefully drop them into the oil. Remove with a slotted spoon as soon as they are crisp and golden, but before they brown. Quickly bring the noodles back to a simmer and divide between three large soup bowls, cover with an equal number of prawns, and dribble sparingly with sesame oil. Eat immediately while still very hot.

Salmon, Teriyake, Somen Noodles

Tender, succulent salmon pieces and
vegetables glazed in *teriyake* sauce float
in a dark, aromatic broth, with a base of
fine *somen* noodles. Serves three to four
people.

225g/8oz dried somen noodles
175g/6oz filleted salmon or salmon steaks
(skinned and boned weight if salmon
*   steaks are used)*
flour
salt and freshly ground black pepper
3 medium-size chestnut or white closed cap
*   mushrooms, stems trimmed*
2 carrots, trimmed and scrubbed
1 large or 2 small leeks, trimmed
2 tbsp Kikkoman's soy sauce
1 tbsp mirin
1 tbsp sake
2 tbsp water
900ml/1 1/2 pints/3 3/4 cups Japanese
*   noodle broth (see page 53)*
2 tbsp peanut oil

Bring a large pan of water to the boil, add
the noodles and cook until nearly *al dente*.
Rinse under cold water and drain. When
drained put them into a large, steep-sided
bowl or soup tureen. Cut the salmon into
small, thin strips. Season enough flour with
salt and pepper to lightly coat the salmon.
Thinly slice the mushrooms. Thinly slice
the vegetables, then stack them in little
piles and cut into *julienne* or matchstick
strips. Boil a small pan of salted water,
plunge the vegetables (but not the mushrooms) into the water, return to the boil
and cook for 30 seconds, then drain.
Combine in a small pan the soy sauce,
mirin, sake and water. Bring to the boil,
then remove from the heat and allow to
cool.

Heat the noodle broth in a covered pan.
Meanwhile, dust the salmon with the seasoned flour. Heat the oil in a wok or non-
stick frying pan. When smoking add the
salmon pieces and stir-fry for 2 minutes.
Remove and drain on absorbent paper.
Pour the hot broth over the noodles and
cover snugly with a large plate to retain
the heat. Quickly re-heat the wok or frying
pan, add the soy, *mirin* and *sake* mixture
and let it bubble. Add the mushrooms and
vegetables, stir for 15 seconds or until
glazed and remove from the heat. Scatter
the salmon pieces and the mushroom and
vegetable mixture over the noodles, and
eat immediately.

Noodle Sukiyaki

A wide array of ingredients may be used for this greatly simplified version of a Japanese favourite, and other vegetables may be substituted for the ones listed. Try, for example, chopped green beans, sprigs of watercress, shredded *daikon* or mooli radish, sliced celery, shredded lettuce etc. Serves two to three people.

12 dried shiitake mushrooms
175g/6oz beef fillet or rump steak
225g/8oz solid bean curd
8 Chinese cabbage leaves
12 fresh spinach leaves
8 baby corn cobs
6 spring onions (scallions)
450g/1lb fresh udon noodles
3 tbsp corn oil
1.75 litres/3 pints/7¹/₂ cups Japanese
* noodle broth (see page 53)*
3 eggs

Soak the mushrooms in a tea cup of hot water for 20 minutes, then remove the hard stems, and thinly slice the caps. Strain the soaking liquid and reserve it. Trim the beef of all fat and cut into small, thin strips. Cut the bean curd into 2cm/³/₄ inch dice. Shred the Chinese cabbage. Trim off the spinach stalks and coarsely shred the leaves. Coarsely chop the corn cobs. Trim the spring onions and, cutting from end to end, slice into long, thin strips. Bring a large pan of water to the boil, add the noodles, return to the boil and cook until *al dente*. Rinse under cold water and drain.

Heat the oil in a small frying pan and quickly seal the beef all over, then remove and drain. Carefully fry the bean curd until pale golden, then remove and drain. Add the corn and the spring onions and stir-fry for 1 minute. Remove and drain on absorbent paper.

Add the mushrooms' soaking liquid to the noodle broth and bring to a simmer in a covered pan. Put the noodles into a large, heat-proof casserole with steep sides. Put the beef, bean curd, fried vegetables, mushrooms, cabbage and spinach on top of the noodles, pour on the broth to give a deep covering and heat the casserole to a simmer. Cook for 3 minutes, then carefully break the eggs into the centre. Cover the cassserole and continue to simmer very gently until the whites have set but before the yolks harden. Serve piping hot.

Udon Noodles in Broth with Char-grilled Salmon and Spinach

Chunks of fresh, char-grilled salmon impart an excellent flavour and texture combined with a little wilted spinach to add a fresh, vivid green colour. Serves two to three people.

450g/1lb fresh udon noodles
175g/6oz fillet of plump, skinned salmon
fine crystal sea salt and freshly ground
  black pepper
2 tbsp olive oil
400ml/14fl oz/1 3/4 cups dashi (see
  page 52) or chicken stock/broth
  (see page 50)
6 tbsp Kikkoman's soy sauce
4 tbsp mirin
2 tsp sugar
175g/6oz fresh spinach, stalks trimmed
3 spring onions (scallions), very thinly
  sliced

In a large pot of salted water, boil the noodles until just *al dente*, then, saving the cooking water, drain and reserve the noodles. Place the salmon on a plate, season and pour the oil over it. Turn the salmon a few times to coat thoroughly in the oil.

Heat a cast-iron griddle or a heavy-bottomed, cast-iron frying pan and, when very hot, place the salmon on the cooking surface. Char both sides lightly (1 minute per side), then remove the griddle or pan from the heat and let the salmon cook gently in the residual heat for about 4 minutes longer on each side; the centre should still be moist but no longer dark pink. (You may have to turn the heat back on to low for the last 2 minutes or so of cooking.) Slice the salmon into 4–6 chunks and keep warm while you make the noodle broth.

Heat in a small pan (but without boiling): the *dashi* or chicken stock, soy sauce, *mirin,* and sugar, stirring to dissolve the granules; remove from the heat but cover the pan to keep the broth warm. Wash the spinach, then immediately throw it into another hot, dry pan. Stir around until wilted, then remove and chop the spinach.

Re-heat the noodles' cooking water and, when boiling, dip in the noodles for just 30 seconds, then immediately drain and put them into a large serving bowl or a soup tureen. Quickly re-heat the stock and pour it over the noodles. Arrange the spring onions, spinach and the salmon chunks on top of the noodles and eat straight away, while still piping hot.

v Noodles in Broth with Courgettes, Tomato and Basil

A delicious soupy noodle dish of the 'East-meets-West' variety, serving four people.

350g/12oz courgettes (zucchini)
1 tbsp peanut oil
3 cloves of garlic, peeled and finely
*   chopped*
1 stick (stalk) of celery, finely diced
3 canned plum tomatoes, crushed
salt and freshly ground black pepper
100g/4oz thin, dried egg noodles
75g/3oz fresh bean sprouts
2–3 fresh chilies, seeded and thinly sliced
1.5 litres/2 1/2 pints/6 1/4 cups vegetable
*   stock/broth (see page 51)*
juice of 1/2 lemon
2 tsp sugar
1 tbsp light soy sauce
3 spring onions (scallions), thinly sliced
12 sweet basil leaves, torn up

Trim off both ends of the courgettes and cut the rest into baton strips (about 5mm/1/4 inch wide and 4cm/1 1/2 inches long). Heat the oil in a small non-stick pan. Stir-fry the garlic and celery over a moderate heat until pale golden but without burning. Add the tomatoes, season lightly and cook over a medium heat for 6–8 minutes until thick and pulpy. Reserve.

Bring a large pan of water to the boil, add the noodles, return to the boil and, stirring to separate the strands, cook until *al dente*, then rinse under cold water and drain. Put the noodles into a soup tureen or a steep-sided serving bowl. Add the bean sprouts, the tomato mixture and chilies, and combine thoroughly.

Heat the stock, lemon juice, and sugar, stirring to dissolve the sugar granules. Add the courgettes, soy sauce and spring onions, and bring to the boil, then cover, reduce the heat and simmer for 4–6 minutes or until the courgettes are just tender but still retain some bite. Pour the mixture over the noodles, stir, sprinkle with basil and eat immediately while piping hot.

Noodles in Broth with Mussels, Lemon Grass and Coriander

A soupier, Oriental version of *linguine alle vongole*, this delicious, fragrant dish should be made with flat ribbon noodles such as Japanese *kishimen*. Serves three people.

900g/2lb mussels (unshelled weight)
225g/8oz kishimen or other dried, wheat ribbon noodles
2 tbsp peanut or corn oil
1 large carrot, scrubbed and finely diced
1 red onion, peeled and chopped
3 cloves of garlic, peeled and finely chopped
2 fresh chilies, seeded and thinly sliced
2 sticks (stalks) of lemon grass, trimmed and thinly sliced
juice of 1/2 lemon
1 wine glass of white wine
400ml/14fl oz/1 3/4 cups dashi (see page 52) or chicken stock/broth (see page 50)
6 tbsp Kikkoman's soy sauce
2 tsp sugar
small handful of fresh coriander (cilantro), chopped

Sort the mussels, discarding any that are not tightly closed, or with cracked shells. Scrub and wash them very thoroughly in several changes of water. Remove any fibre and beard.

Bring abundant water to the boil. Add the noodles, return to the boil and cook until just *al dente*. Rinse under cold water and drain.

Heat the oil to smoking point in a large pan. Add the carrot, onion, garlic, chilies and lemon grass, and stir-fry for 2–3 minutes. Pour in the lemon juice, wine, *dashi* or chicken stock, the soy sauce and sugar. Stirring to dissolve the granules, bring to the boil, then add the cleaned and sorted mussels, mix, cover tightly and cook for 15 minutes, initially over a high heat then at a simmer. With a slotted spoon or strainer, remove the mussels, leaving the other ingredients behind in the pan, and discard any whose shells have not opened wide. Remove the meats from the good shells, and return them to the pan. Add the drained noodles and the coriander, heat thoroughly, then tip into a soup tureen or serving bowl and serve straight away,

Home-made Stocks

Although busy cooks should not hesitate to use cubes or commercial liquid stocks, for flavour and a rich consistency home-made stock cannot be bettered. By making your own you also avoid unwanted additives such as colourings and the flavour enhancer monosodium glutamate which, unfortunately, are present in most proprietary stock cubes. You can refrigerate the stocks for a couple of days or even pour them into freezer bags. Tightly sealed, they will freeze perfectly (thaw thoroughly before using). Another well-tried technique, which is especially useful when only small amounts are needed, is to pour the stock into ice-cube trays and freeze. That way, you can use as much or as little as you need. All three of the following recipes produce rich, well-flavoured stocks.

. . . .

Simple Beef Stock (Broth)

2 tbsp olive oil
225g/8oz piece of beef, preferably with
    some bone, fat removed
1 large onion, peeled and chopped
1 carrot, scrubbed and chopped
white part of 2 cleaned leeks, trimmed and
    chopped
2 celery sticks (stalks), chopped
small bunch of fresh parsley (stalks and
    leaves)
2 bay leaves
2 cloves
salt
1 tsp black peppercorns
2 litres/3 1/2 pints/8 3/4 cups water
1 tbsp dark soy sauce

Heat the oil in a large pan. Brown the beef, then add the vegetables, herbs, spices and seasoning down to and including the peppercorns. Stir around for a few minutes, until the bottom of the pan begins to brown. (This will ensure a good dark-coloured stock.) Add the water and bring to the boil, then reduce the heat and simmer, skimming off all the scum as it rises. Cover, and after 1 1/2–2 hours the stock should be ready. Add the soy sauce, mix and allow to cool, spoon off any fat and strain. Refrigerate or freeze until required.

Rich Chicken Stock (Broth)

1 raw chicken carcass, preferably with
*   some meat left on but skinned*
1 large onion, peeled and chopped
2 cleaned leeks, trimmed and chopped
2 celery sticks (stalks), chopped
small bunch of fresh parsley (stalks and
*   leaves)*
1 bay leaf
salt
12 black peppercorns
2 litres/3 1/2 pints/8 3/4 cups water

Put all the ingredients into a very large
pan, pour in the water and bring to the
boil. Cover, reduce the heat and simmer,
skimming off all the scum as it rises. After
about 2 hours the stock will be ready.
Allow it to cool, spoon off any fat and
strain. Refrigerate or freeze until required.

v Well-flavoured Vegetable Stock (Broth)

4 tbsp olive oil
2 onions, peeled and chopped
4 cleaned leeks, trimmed and chopped
4 carrots, scrubbed and chopped
4 celery sticks (stalks), chopped
8 parsley stalks with their leaves
1 bay leaf
1 tbsp tomato purée (paste)
salt
12 black peppercorns
2 litres/3 1/2 pints/8 3/4 cups water
1 tbsp Worcester sauce or light soy sauce

Put everything except for the Worcester or soy sauce into a large pan and bring to the boil. Cover, reduce the heat and simmer for 1 hour, skimming if necessary. Add the Worcester or soy sauce, mix, and check the seasoning. Strain and refrigerate or freeze.

Note: vegetarians should not use Worcester sauce.

Home-made Dashi

This is a standard, basic, home-made recipe for *dashi*. Some Japanese recipes specify dried sardines, but you may omit the dried fish altogether for a very light stock. You will have to go to a Japanese supermarket or food shop to find the dried ingredients or they may be obtained by mail order (see page 141 for details). This makes 1 litre/1 3/4 pints/4 1/3 cups. Although *dashi* granules may be used for convenience, they contain monosodium glutamate, to which many people have an unpleasant reaction. (If you are using the granules use 3 tsp to 600ml/1 pint/2 1/2 cups boiling water, multiplying upwards as required.)

1 litre/1 3/4 pints/4 1/3 cups cold water
25g/1oz dried giant kelp (konbu)
25g/1oz dried bonito flakes (han-katsuo)

Put the water and kelp into a pan and heat. Before the water boils but after several minutes at a gentle simmer, remove the kelp. Bring the liquid to the boil, then add a little additional cold water, followed by the bonito flakes. Return to the boil, then immediately remove from the heat. Rest for a minute or two, then strain the liquid. May be refrigerated for a day or two.

Note: once cooked the kelp and bonito flakes may be re-used; they can be simmered, uncovered, in the same volume of cold water for 20–30 minutes to produce a much more concentrated version of *dashi*.

Japanese Noodle Broth

Although bottled, ready-made broth concentrate is good and convenient, an excellent mixture can be made easily at home. This standard recipe makes 2.25 litres/4 pints/10 cups of noodle broth which, stored in a sealed container, will keep for a few days in the fridge. Allow 900ml/1¹/2 pints/3 ³/4 cups of broth for 225g/8oz dried noodles – enough for two people.

2.25 litres/4 pints/10 cups dashi (see page 52)
2 tsp salt
120ml/4fl oz/¹/2 cup Kikkoman's soy sauce
2 tbsp sugar
3 tbsp mirin

Put all the ingredients into a pot and bring to a simmer. If you are going to use the broth the same day, set aside after it has simmered for a minute or two, and simmer again briefly when required. Otherwise, let it cool, cover and refrigerate; alternatively, freeze the broth in plastic freezer bags.

COLD NOODLE DISHES AND NOODLE SALADS

Noodles make exceptionally interesting salads with many possible variations, combining hot, sweet, sour and salty flavours. In fact a wide range of ingredients from throughout the south-east Asian region are represented in this chapter: peanuts, lime juice, soy sauce, fish sauce, rice vinegar, sesame oil, chilies, garlic, shallots, spring onions (scallions), fresh mint and coriander (cilantro) all lend their zesty accents to many of the ensuing recipes.

Most, if not all noodle varieties are suitable for delicious salads, but the most unusual are cellophane or bean thread noodles. Their startling slippery texture and transparent appearance give them a special quality, and their subtle, delicate flavour gives them the ability to absorb powerful added flavours.

Salads such as *Soba noodles with dipping sauce* are especially refreshing in hot weather, even if the *wasabi* gives a hot pungency to the chilled noodles. My favourite noodle salads include: *Cold sesame noodles with delicious, crunchy cucumber and bean sprouts*; *Noodle salad with pickled vegetables*; *Hot and spicy vegetable and noodle salad* (really more of a curry); the rich *Gado-gado egg noodles*; *Simple summer salad,* with its nutty garnish of toasted sesame seeds and cool grated radish; and a dish I created by marrying east and west called *Warm salad of char-grilled egg 'oil' noodles with charred lamb and red chilies*. However, pride of place goes to the delicious, Vietnamese-inspired *Noodle salad with lettuce and chili-beef cups*, a wonderful dish packed with contrasting textures and flavours.

Soba Noodles with Dipping Sauce

In Japan, this noodle dish is normally served chilled, in bamboo baskets. There are several different toppings, but here I suggest finely chopped spring onions, shredded *daikon* or mooli radish, and watercress or spinach. Grated, fresh *wasabi* is usually added. This is a pungent, hot-tasting root that is similar, though unrelated, to our own horseradish. Outside Japan, fresh *wasabi* is unobtainable but *wasabi* paste can be bought in plastic tubes resembling toothpaste. This recipe serves two to three people.

175g/6oz dried soba noodles
white part of 4 spring onions (scallions),
*   finely chopped*
9cm/3¹/2 inch piece of daikon or mooli
*   radish, peeled and coarsely grated*
small handful of fresh watercress or fresh
*   spinach, stalks removed, shredded*
1–2 tsp wasabi paste, or to taste
600ml/1 pint/2¹/2 cups noodle dipping
*   sauce (see the next recipe), chilled*

Bring a large pan of water to the boil, add the noodles, return to the boil and cook until *al dente*, then rinse under cold water and drain thoroughly. Put the noodles into a soup tureen or a steep-sided bowl. When ready to eat, place the vegetables on top of the noodles, add the *wasabi*, moisten with a little chilled noodle dipping sauce and serve the rest of the dipping sauce in a separate bowl.

Dipping Sauce for Soba Noodles

The addition of dried bonito flakes (*han-katsuo*) is indispensable to this delicious dipping sauce. They may be obtained, packed in plastic bags, in Japanese shops. Sainsbury's have recently introduced this and many other Japanese ingredients, including dried noodles, into their leading branches.

350ml/12fl oz/1¹/2 cups dashi
  (see page 52)
120ml/4fl oz/¹/2 cup dark soy sauce
3 tbsp Kikkoman's soy sauce
2 tbsp mirin
1 tbsp sake
1 tsp sugar
1 tsp salt
15g/¹/2oz dried bonito flakes

Put everything except for the bonito flakes into a small pan and bring to the boil, stirring, then remove from the heat. Add the bonito flakes, stir for 30 seconds off the heat, then strain into a clean container. Allow to cool and use the same day or seal and store in the fridge.

. . . .

Dipping sauce made with noodle broth concentrate

Noodle broth concentrate comes in glass or plastic bottles. To make dipping sauce, dilute 1 part concentrate in 1–2 parts water.

Simple Summer Noodle Salad

This simple recipe is adapted from traditional Japanese *soba* noodle salads. It is quite delicate but with a delightful nutty taste and a subtle pungency imparted by the *wasabi*. A pleasantly refreshing light lunch for hot days, which serves two to three people.

225g/8oz dried soba noodles
4 tbsp soba concentrate/noodle broth
   concentrate
175ml/6fl oz/³/4 cup dashi (see page 52)
   or chicken stock/broth (see page 50)
1/2 tbsp mirin
white part of 2 spring onions (scallions),
   very thinly sliced
3 tsp wasabi
5cm/2 inch piece of daikon or mooli radish
   peeled and grated
2 tsp sesame seeds, lightly toasted in a very
   hot, dry pan

Bring abundant water to the boil, add the noodles and cook until *al dente*. Rinse under cold water, drain and chill in the fridge. Put into a small pan the concentrate, the *dashi* or stock, and the *mirin*. Bring to a simmer and cook for 1 minute, then allow to cool and chill in the fridge.

When nearly ready to eat, divide the noodles into two or three serving portions and place on plates. Pour the dipping sauce into individual small bowls. Divide and add the spring onions, *wasabi* and radish. Mix. Scatter the sesame seeds over the noodles and serve with the dipping sauce.

v Noodle Salad with Bean Curd and Watercress

This colourful salad is based on Madhur Jaffrey's Taiwanese recipe for 'Bean curd with fresh coriander', published in *Eastern Vegetarian Cookery* (Jonathan Cape 1983). Don't be put off by the amount of chilies since the large varieties are relatively mild. Alternatively, use just 1 or 2 small, hot chilies and 1/4 sweet red pepper.

175g/6oz cellophane noodles
4 large, dried red chilies
1 tsp corn flour
4 tbsp water
1 tbsp light soy sauce
1 tbsp yellow bean sauce
2 tbsp peanut oil
1/2 tsp salt
1/2 tsp sugar
175g/6oz solid bean curd, cut into
    2cm/3/4 inch cubes
10 sprigs of watercress, stems trimmed
small handful of fresh coriander (cilantro),
    chopped

Soak the cellophane noodles and chilies in a covering of hot water until soft (about 5 minutes), then drain. Put the noodles in a serving bowl. De-seed and thinly slice the chilies.

Meanwhile, dissolve the corn flour in the water, adding the soy and yellow bean sauces. Heat the oil to smoking point in a wok. Add the chilies, salt, and sugar, and stir-fry for 30 seconds. Add the bean curd cubes, reduce the heat and stir for 1 minute taking care not to break them. Stir the sauce mixture and pour it over the bean curd. Raise the heat again and cook until the liquid thickens slightly. Add the watercress and coriander and cook until slightly wilted – about 20 seconds longer. Pour the wok contents over the noodles and serve at room temperature.

Cellophane Noodle Salad with Bean Sprouts and Sweet and Sour Dipping Sauce

This quick and easy dish makes a refreshing but nutritious vegetarian salad, and can be served with other Oriental dishes or just on its own. The translucent noodles have a delightfully silky texture and, since both the noodles and the bean sprouts are the product of mung beans they seem an appropriate partnership. It may be eaten as soon as the bean sprouts have cooled to room temperature; alternatively, the salad can be chilled lightly in the fridge. Serves three to four people.

175g/6oz cellophane noodles
1 tbsp sugar
2 tbsp rice vinegar
2 tbsp Kikkoman's soy sauce
1 tbsp fish sauce
3 fresh chilies, seeded and very thinly
   sliced
leaves from 6 sprigs of fresh coriander
   (cilantro)
1 tbsp peanut oil
2 cloves of garlic, peeled and thinly sliced
1 cm/1/2 inch piece of fresh ginger, peeled
   and finely chopped
white part of 4 spring onions (scallions),
   sliced
225g/8oz fresh bean sprouts
10cm/4 inch section of cucumber, peeled
   and cut into matchstick strips

Soak the cellophane noodles in very hot (not boiling) water until soft (about 5 minutes), then rinse and drain them. Meanwhile, dissolve the sugar with the vinegar, soy and fish sauces. Add the chilies and coriander and set aside: this is the dipping sauce.

Heat the oil to smoking point in a wok, add the garlic, ginger, and the white part of the spring onions. Stir-fry for 30 seconds, then add the bean sprouts. Stir-fry for 30 seconds longer, then tip the wok contents into a serving bowl.

Cut the noodles into sections roughly the same length as the bean sprouts and add them to the bowl together with the cucumber strips. Mix thoroughly and allow to cool or refrigerate for up to 2 hours. Just before serving moisten the salad with a little dipping sauce and serve the rest in a separate bowl.

v Cellophane Noodle Salad with Rainbow Vegetables and Peanut Dressing

This pretty, very colourful salad is a complete and nourishing meal in its own right. Do experiment with other raw and cooked vegetable combinations for equally rewarding results. It will serve up to six people with other dishes, or as an appetizer.

175g/6oz cellophane noodles
1 tbsp sesame oil
2 cloves of garlic, peeled and finely chopped
50g/2oz button mushrooms, sliced
1 small carrot, scrubbed and finely diced
1/2 red pepper, seeded, de-pithed and finely diced
1/2 green pepper, seeded, de-pithed and finely diced
75g/3oz baby corn, coarsely chopped
1 tbsp Shaohsing wine
75g/3oz frozen peas, thawed
large handful of young spinach, lower stems trimmed, coarsely chopped
2 tbsp peanut oil
1 egg plus 1 egg yolk, beaten
75g/3oz roasted peanuts, lightly crushed
2 tsp sugar
1/4–1/2 tsp cayenne or to taste
1 tbsp rice vinegar
1 tbsp light soy sauce
1 tbsp dark soy sauce
3 spring onions (scallions), trimmed and thinly sliced
5cm/2 inch section of cucumber, peeled and very thinly sliced

Soak the cellophane noodles in very hot water until soft, then rinse under cold water and drain.

Heat the sesame oil in a wok, add the garlic, mushrooms, carrot, peppers and baby corn and stir-fry for 2 minutes, then add the Shaohsing wine and peas and cook for 1 minute, add the spinach and stir for 1 minute longer. Remove and set aside in a large bowl.

Clean and dry the wok and heat 1 tbsp peanut oil to smoking point. Pour in the beaten egg and make an omelette. Drain the omelette on absorbent paper and slice into thin strips.

Mix together half the crushed peanuts, the sugar, cayenne, 1 tbsp peanut oil, the vinegar, and soy sauces. Arrange the noodles on a serving platter, put the cooked and raw vegetables on top and pour over the peanut dressing. Scatter the omelette strips on top and sprinkle with the remaining nuts. Serve with additional soy sauce, if desired.

Cold Sesame Noodles

These deliciously spicy noodles from northern China are very simple to make, and all the ingredients are easily obtained. Only the bacon and aromatic ingredients need quick cooking, and of course the noodles need a short boil to soften them, but the rest is mere assembly. Although it is traditional to include chunks of fatty roast pork, which the Chinese adore, morsels of back bacon, grilled until crisp around the edges, are very tasty, give a better texture and are certainly much more appealing! This serves two to three people on its own or four to six people with other Chinese dishes. The noodles taste best of all when left for a few hours to absorb the flavourings.

50g/2oz lean back bacon
1 tbsp peanut oil
1cm/1/2 inch piece of fresh ginger, finely
    chopped
1 clove of garlic, peeled and thinly sliced
100g/4oz fresh bean sprouts
2 tsp Shaohsing wine
18cm/7 inch section of cucumber, peeled
225g/8oz dried egg noodles
2 spring onions (scallions), very thinly
    sliced
3 tbsp sesame oil
1 1/2 tbsp light soy sauce
1 tsp chili sauce
plenty of freshly ground black pepper
1 tsp sugar
1/2 tsp salt

Grill (broil) the bacon until the edges crisp up, then cut it up into very small pieces. Heat the peanut oil in a wok to smoking point, then add the ginger, garlic and bean sprouts. Stir-fry for 30 seconds, splash in the Shaohsing wine and toss for 30 seconds longer. Scoop into a small bowl and leave to cool.

Cut the cucumber in half lengthways, scoop out and discard the seedy centre and finely slice the flesh. Chop into small dice and set aside.

Boil the noodles until *al dente*, or as directed by the packet instructions, separating the strands with a wooden spoon, then rinse them under cold water and drain thoroughly. Combine all the ingredients in a serving bowl, mixing very thoroughly. May be served straight away or refrigerated for up to 6 hours.

v Noodle Salad with Pickled Vegetables

This unusual vegetarian noodle salad was inspired by Yan Kit So's recipe for 'Cantonese pickled vegetables' from her *Classic Chinese Cookbook* (Dorling Kindersley, 1984). By pepping up the flavourings and combining the lightly pickled raw vegetables with noodles, I have created an excellent new dish which works best as an appetizer for four to six people. Plan ahead to allow for the salting and chilling phases, but otherwise enjoy the simplicity and speed of preparation. This is healthy, warm-weather eating at its best, and packs plenty of flavour.

10cm/4 inch section of cucumber, peeled
3 carrots, scrubbed
2 celery sticks (stalks)
4 Chinese cabbage leaves
2 fresh chilies, seeded
2 spring onions (scallions), trimmed
1 tsp salt
2 tbsp sugar
2 tbsp rice vinegar
1 tbsp light soy sauce
175g/6oz thin dried egg noodles
freshly ground black pepper
1¹/2 tbsp sesame oil

Cut the cucumber down the middle, from top to bottom. With a teaspoon, scoop out and discard the seedy middle part. Cut the cucumber, carrots and celery at a diagonal angle into 5mm/¹/4 inch sections. Coarsely chop the cabbage. Thinly slice the chilies and spring onions. Put into a large colander all the vegetables except for the chilies and spring onions, and sprinkle with the salt. Leave for 1–3 hours, then rinse and pat them dry. Put all the vegetables into a glass or ceramic bowl. Dissolve the sugar in the vinegar and soy sauce. Pour the mixture over the vegetables, combine thoroughly and refrigerate for at least 30 minutes but preferably 2 hours as they should be well chilled.

When you are nearly ready to eat, boil the noodles in abundant water until *al dente*, separating the strands with a wooden spoon. Plunge into cold water, then drain thoroughly. Add the noodles to the bowl containing the pickled vegetables, sprinkle with black pepper and sesame oil, and combine very thoroughly. Eat cold.

Noodle Salad with Lettuce and Chili-Beef Cups

This delicious noodle salad with Vietnamese-inspired flavours serves two to three people.

225g/8oz beef sirloin or rump steak, trimmed
175g/6oz thin, dried egg noodles
2¹/₂ tbsp peanut oil
1 Cos (romaine) lettuce heart or 1 'little gem' lettuce
2 large or 4 small shallots, peeled and sliced
3 cloves of garlic, peeled and finely chopped
2 fresh chilies, seeded and cut into long, thin strips
1 tbsp light soy sauce
1 tbsp fish sauce
2 tsp sugar
juice of 1 lime
50g/2oz roasted peanuts, lightly crushed
white part of 2 spring onions (scallions), thinly sliced
leaves from 6 sprigs of coriander (cilantro), chopped
leaves from 4 sprigs of mint, chopped
2 tbsp dark soy sauce

Cut the beef into large, even-sized cubes, put in the freezer for at least 15 minutes to firm up but without allowing the meat to freeze: this is to facilitate wafer-thin slicing.

Meanwhile, bring a large pan of water to the boil, add the noodles, return to the boil and cook until *al dente*. Rinse under cold water, drain and toss in 2 tsp of the oil. Place the noodles on a large serving platter. Separate the lettuce into individual cup-shaped leaves. Reserve the largest leaves, shred the smaller ones and arrange them in a ring around the noodles. With a very sharp knife, slice the beef as thinly as possible.

Heat the remaining 2 tbsp oil to smoking point in a wok, add the shallots, garlic and chilies and stir-fry for just 30 seconds. Add the beef, stir once and pour in the light soy and fish sauces. Toss for just 1¹/₂ minutes or until the meat no longer looks raw, then add the sugar, and mix.

Transfer the wok contents to a bowl. When the beef morsels are cool put them in the lettuce leaf cups, pour over the juices from the bowl, sprinkle with the lime juice, crushed peanuts, spring onions, herbs, and dark soy sauce to taste. Place the lettuce cups on top of the noodles and serve.

v Noodle Salad with Vegetables and Sesame-Soy Dressing

This recipe is inspired by Madhur Jaffrey's 'Noodles with a soy-sauce dressing', from her book *Eastern Vegetarian Cooking* (Jonathan Cape, 1983). I have sharpened the dressing, adding nutty toasted sesame seeds and a few fiery drops of chili oil. I have also added carrot and watercress for extra colour and a little more crunch. A delicious salad serving two to three people, which may be made in advance.

225g/8oz thin, dried egg noodles
2 tbsp sesame oil
1 heaped tbsp sesame seeds, lightly toasted
   in a very hot, dry pan
2 tbsp light soy sauce
1 tbsp dark soy sauce
1 tbsp rice vinegar
1 clove garlic, peeled and crushed
1 tsp sugar
1/2–1tsp chili oil, or to taste
2 carrots, scrubbed and coarsely grated
into a bowl of water to prevent
   discolouring
100g/4oz bean sprouts
2 'little gem' lettuces, shredded
small handful of watercress

Bring a large pan of water to the boil, add the noodles, return to the boil and cook until *al dente*. Rinse under cold water and drain. Toss with 1 tbsp sesame oil and place the noodles on a large serving dish.

   Put the toasted sesame seeds in a bowl, add the remaining sesame oil, soy sauces, rice vinegar, garlic, sugar, and chili oil. Mix thoroughly, stirring to dissolve the sugar granules, and leave to infuse for at least 15 minutes. Meanwhile, drain the carrot and pat dry with absorbent paper. Place the vegetables in individual heaps surrounding the noodles. Stir the dressing and pour over the noodles. Serve the salad cold or chilled.

Hot and Spicy Vegetable and Noodle Salad

This delicious dish is based on Vatcharin Bhumichitr's 'Nam prik curry noodles' from his *Thai Cookbook* (Pavilion, 1994). I have simplified his excellent though elaborate, authentic recipe and changed some of the ingredients, most significantly substituting fresh 'oil' noodles for rice noodles. (Alternatively, use 225g/8oz dried, thick egg noodles, boiled until *al dente*, rinsed and drained. They should then be fried as described in the recipe.) Frying the noodles first gives a lot of extra flavour. This is both a curry and a salad, since the spicy curry sauce is used as a dressing for both the noodles and the accompanying blanched vegetables, which are served tepid or cold. Although not strictly vegetarian, replace the fish sauce with light soy sauce to make it a vegetarian recipe. This serves two to three people if eaten as a snack or light meal, though you may find the dish too delicious to stretch that far!

2 tsp peanut oil
450g/1lb fresh 'oil' noodles
100g/4oz yardlong or green beans, trimmed and chopped into 1cm/¹/2 inch sections
100g/4oz fresh, young, leaf spinach, coarsely chopped
110g/4oz bean sprouts
2 tbsp corn oil
1 small onion, peeled, halved from top to bottom, and thinly sliced
6 peeled cloves of garlic, 2 of them thinly sliced and 4 left whole
2 large, dried red chilies, coarsely chopped
4 large shallots, peeled and chopped
4 coriander (cilantro) roots, cleaned
6 fresh or dried, extra hot chilies
2 sticks (stalks) of lemon grass, trimmed, outer layer removed, chopped
3 tbsp water
1 tbsp Thai 'red' curry paste
1 tbsp sugar
juice of 1 lime
1 tbsp fish sauce
1 tbsp light soy sauce
450ml/15fl oz/2 cups canned coconut milk
small handful of fresh coriander, chopped

Heat 2 tsp peanut oil in a large, non-stick frying pan, add the noodles, press them down with a spatula and fry until the base is golden-brown in patches. Turn the noodles as best you can and repeat, then remove and arrange on a large serving platter.

Bring a pan of water to the boil, add the beans and boil until just tender. Drain and refresh in cold water. Throw the spinach into the damp pan, stir briefly over a high heat until wilted, and remove. Arrange the cooked vegetables and the raw bean sprouts in small heaps surrounding the noodles.

Heat 1 tbsp corn oil to smoking point in the non-stick frying pan. Fry the onion and sliced garlic until lightly browned, remove with a slotted spoon and drain on absorbent paper. Re-heat the oil and briefly fry the dried chili pieces; remove as soon as they darken.

Put into a food processor or mortar, the shallots, whole garlic cloves, coriander roots, hot chilies, lemon grass, and water. Process or pound to a paste.

Pour the remaining 1 tbsp corn oil into the frying pan, heat and add the 'red' curry paste. Stir for a few seconds to release aroma, then add the sugar, lime juice, fish and soy sauces, and the coconut milk. Stir in the freshly-made paste and simmer for about 6 minutes to thicken the curry slightly, then stir in the fried chilies, fried onion, garlic, and coriander. Pour the curry sauce over the noodles and serve tepid or cold.

v Gado-Gado Egg Noodles

Gado-gado is the name of an Indonesian salad with a rich and spicy peanut dressing. The idea of using noodles as the base for a hearty *gado-gado* salad came to me one evening out of the blue, and the results, I hope you will agree, are delicious! This dish is quite substantial, and serves four people.

675g/1¹/₂lbs fresh egg noodles
4 tbsp peanut oil

AT LEAST 4 OF THE FOLLOWING:
50g/2oz sliced bamboo shoots (canned ones are fine), rinsed and drained
50g/2oz canned water chestnuts, rinsed, drained and quartered
1 lettuce heart, washed and coarsely shredded
50g/2oz Chinese leaf cabbage, coarsely chopped
100g/4oz piece of cucumber, peeled and diced
50g/2oz fresh bean sprouts
50g/2oz cherry tomatoes, washed and cut in half
50g/2oz piece of daikon or mouli radish, washed and cubed
1 small green pepper, washed, seeded and diced

PEANUT SAUCE
1 red onion, peeled and finely chopped
3 cloves of garlic, peeled and finely chopped
2–3 fresh chilies, seeded and thinly sliced
75g/3oz roasted peanuts, crushed in a food processor
2 tsp Thai 'red' curry paste
250ml/8fl oz/1 cup canned coconut milk
2 tbsp soy sauce
1 tbsp sugar
1 tsp cayenne
¹/₂ tsp turmeric

TO GARNISH
1 lemon or 2 limes, quartered or halved; small handful of fresh coriander (cilantro) or basil, washed and chopped; 1 or 2 hard-boiled (hard-cooked) eggs, peeled and quartered or sliced

Bring a large pan of water to the boil, immerse the fresh egg noodles, bring back to the boil, and cook until *al dente*. Rinse and drain. Toss them with 1 tbsp of the oil and the vegetables. Turn the noodles and vegetables on to a large, wide serving platter, mixing thoroughly. The peanut sauce will be poured over them.

Now make the peanut sauce. Heat the rest of the oil in a saucepan. When just smoking, add the onion, garlic and chilies. Stir-fry until soft and golden, then add the peanuts and the curry paste and stir-fry for a couple of minutes longer. Now pour in the coconut milk and 120ml/4fl oz/$\frac{1}{2}$ cup water, soy sauce, and add the sugar,

cayenne and turmeric. Mix well and simmer for about 20 minutes or until the oil separates from the sauce. Let the sauce cool to room temperature, then pour half of it over the noodles. Sprinkle with the garnishes and serve with a bowl of the remaining peanut sauce, to which your guests may help themselves.

Variations:
Carrots, green beans, mangetouts (snow peas), small new potatoes, broccoli or cauliflower, all cut into small chunks and boiled until just tender, may be substituted for the raw vegetables. Best of all is a combination of boiled and raw vegetables.

Warm Salad of Char-grilled Egg 'Oil' Noodles with Charred Lamb and Red Chilies

I created this excellent, smoky-flavoured dish by marrying together Oriental and Mediterranean techniques and ingredients. Unless the noodles themselves are quite oily and also tossed through in oil prior to being charred on the hot surface, they may stick to the pan. For that reason, and also because their plump, soft texture suits the dish best, I strongly recommend that you only use the yellow egg 'oil' noodles sold in plastic bags in Chinese supermarkets. The charred chilies may be very hot unless you scrape out the seeds before you eat them. Serves two to three people.

3 large, dried red chilies

6 prime lamb cutlets

4 cloves of garlic, peeled and crushed

1cm/1/2 inch piece of fresh ginger, peeled and finely chopped

tender part of 2 sticks (stalks) of lemon grass

1 tbsp rice vinegar

3 tsp sesame oil

freshly ground black pepper

3 fresh, very ripe plum or vine tomatoes, peeled and finely diced (canned plum tomatoes will do)

1 fresh chili pepper, seeded and finely chopped

white part of 3 spring onions (scallions), chopped

1/2 tsp sugar

1/2 tsp salt

small handful of fresh coriander (cilantro), chopped

3 tbsp olive oil

450g/1lb fresh egg 'oil' noodles

Soak the chili peppers in a cup of hot water for about 15 minutes. Remove the lean meat from the surrounding fat and bone and cut into thin strips about 4cm/ 1¹/₂ inches long. Put the lamb in a bowl, add the garlic, ginger, lemon grass, rice vinegar, sesame oil and plenty of black pepper. Combine thoroughly, cover, and set aside for at least 30 minutes, but preferably 1 hour.

Meanwhile, combine in a bowl the tomatoes, the chopped fresh chili, spring onions, sugar, salt, coriander and 2 tbsp olive oil. Mix thoroughly and set aside.

Heat a large, heavy-bottomed cast-iron frying pan until very hot. Meanwhile, remove the peppers from their soaking water, drain and pat them dry with absorbent paper. Place the peppers in the hot frying pan and, shaking the pan from time to time, char until blackened in patches; they should not burn. Remove and set aside.

Put the noodles in a bowl and toss with the remaining olive oil. Remove the lamb from the marinade, scrape off the clinging marinade bits and re-heat the pan. Add the lamb and stir around until browned: this will take next to no time if the pan is very hot, as it should be. Remove the lamb to a warmed bowl and cover to keep warm. With tongs or your fingers, pick up half the noodles and put them into the hot pan. Spread the noodles and press down with the back of a spatula to flatten them. Char until the base noodles have some dark brown spots, then scrape the bottom of the pan, lift with a spatula and turn, but don't worry if the noodles do not char evenly or if some do stick. Press down to char the other side, then remove and repeat for the remaining noodles. While the noodles cook, heat the tomato mixture in a small pan until bubbling and thick.

Arrange the noodles on a warmed serving platter. Spoon the tomato mixture over them and scatter the lamb on top. Garnish with the whole charred chilies and serve warm or at room temperature.

Noodles with Spicy Meatballs

This is my hot and zesty Oriental-style version of spaghetti with meatballs, and an excellent dish it is at that! Serves two or three people.

450g/1lb lean, minced (ground) beef or
  pork
4 cloves of garlic, peeled and finely
  chopped
2 fresh, green chilies, finely chopped
2 tsp Moroccan ground mixed spice or
  garam masala
generous handful of fresh coriander
  (cilantro), finely chopped
salt and freshly ground black pepper
1 tbsp light soy sauce
5 tbsp peanut or corn oil
a little flour to coat the meatballs
3–4 small, extra hot dried chilies, crumbled
400g/14oz canned plum tomatoes, chopped
225g/8oz medium, dried egg noodles

Combine in a bowl the minced meat, two thirds of the garlic, the fresh chilies, the spice or garam masala, half the chopped fresh coriander, a little salt and pepper, the soy sauce and 1 tbsp of the oil. Shape the mixture into golf balls. Heat 2 tbsp oil in a non-stick frying pan. Meanwhile, roll the meatballs in flour to give a light coating. Fry them gently in batches until they are lightly browned all over (about 7 minutes). Transfer to a plate lined with absorbent paper.

Heat the remaining oil in a pan. Add the rest of the garlic and the dried chilies and mix. Add the tomatoes, and season with salt and pepper. Cook, uncovered, over a medium heat for 8 minutes, or until thick. Add the meatballs to the sauce, cover the pan and simmer for a further 15–20 minutes. Add a little water if the sauce is too dry, and turn the meatballs from time to time.

Meanwhile, bring a large pot of water to the boil, add the noodles, return to the boil and, stirring to separate the strands, cook until al dente. Drain and arrange in a serving bowl. Add the remaining coriander to the pan with the meatballs and serve them, with their sauce, over the noodles. Eat warm or at room temperature.

STIR-FRIED AND DEEP-FRIED NOODLE DISHES

When stir-fried with a small quantity of meat, seafood or poultry, plenty of fresh, lightly cooked vegetables, and tangy exotic flavourings, noodles make the perfect, quickly-cooked meal. Deep-fried rice and egg noodles make a crisp, savoury base for rich, saucy toppings.

Many classic Oriental dishes are included. From Thailand come *Pad Thai*, *Mee krob*, and *Fried rice noodles with tiger prawns and vegetables*. Among the many Chinese-inspired dishes are *Noodles dressed with ginger and spring onions*, *Noodles with mussels and black beans*, the various *Chow mein* recipes, *Fried egg noodles with water chestnuts*, *Noodles with minced pork in black bean sauce*, *Szechwan-style noodles*, and the much more modern *Noodles with asparagus and lettuce in chili bean sauce*. Japan provides delicious *Yaki-soba noodles in a spicy sauce*, Korea, a subtle *Noodle stir-fry with beef and vegetables*, and some interesting stir-fries from Indonesia and Singapore are also included.

There are many possible variations, and several recipes that combine European and Oriental ingredients to great effect such as acorn squash, fresh plum tomatoes and basil; oyster mushrooms, prawns (shrimp) and alfalfa sprouts; chicken with allspice and sweet red pepper; smoked bacon, broccoli and sesame seeds; and beef, green pepper and asparagus, to name but a few.

The following dishes will all repay experimentation with different combinations of ingredients, and once you have mastered the essential techniques of stir-frying and deep-frying, there is no limit to the delicious noodle dishes you can create for yourself.

Noodles Dressed with Ginger and Spring Onions

This popular and ubiquitous Chinese noodle dish is also one of the most simple to prepare. In fact, it is the perfect quick snack or light lunch, and you can make it suitable for a vegetarian if you omit the oyster sauce. My version is slightly more pungent than usual, with a little extra kick from garlic and chili. Serves two to three people.

225g/8oz dried egg noodles
8 spring onions (scallions), trimmed
2cm/3/4 inch piece of fresh ginger, peeled
1 clove of garlic, peeled
1 green chili, seeded
3 tbsp peanut oil
1/2 tsp salt
1/2 tsp sugar
1 tbsp oyster sauce
1 tbsp light soy sauce
2 tsp sesame oil

Bring a large pan of water to the boil, add the egg noodles and, stirring to separate the strands, cook until *al dente*, then rinse under cold water and drain. Meanwhile chop the white part of the spring onions finely, and thinly slice the green parts. Chop the ginger, garlic and chili finely.

Heat the peanut oil to smoking point, add the ginger, garlic, white part of the spring onions and chili and toss for 15-30 seconds. Add the salt and sugar, mix, then put the noodles, oyster and soy sauces into the wok. Toss to coat and heat through, transfer to a warmed serving dish, sprinkle with the green part of the spring onions and the sesame oil, and eat immediately.

Notes: Scattered morsels of crisp bacon over the noodles make an even tastier version. You could accompany these noodles, and many others in this book, with a salad of shredded Chinese leaf cabbage or lettuce, dressed with a delicious Oriental vinaigrette. Mix together 1 tbsp each of light soy sauce, rice vinegar, sesame oil, toasted sesame seeds; a crushed garlic clove; and cayenne to taste.

[v] Noodles with Asparagus and Lettuce in Chili Bean Sauce

Here is a simple, Chinese-inspired vegetarian noodle dish, which makes a complete hot and savoury meal for two people.

225g/8oz dried egg noodles
1 bundle asparagus (about 225g/8oz)
2 cloves of garlic, peeled and finely
    chopped
2 chilies, seeded and chopped
1 tbsp sesame oil
1 tbsp light soy sauce
3 tsp Shaohsing wine
2 tsp chili bean sauce
1/2 tsp salt
1/2 tsp sugar
3 tbsp peanut oil
120ml/4fl oz/1/2 cup vegetable stock/broth
    (see page 51)
1 lettuce heart or 'little gem' lettuce,
    quartered

Bring a large pan of water to the boil. Put in the noodles and cook until *al dente* or according to the packet instructions, then rinse and drain well. Snap off the tough asparagus bottoms, then slice at a slight diagonal into 2cm/3/4 inch sections. In a bowl mix together the garlic, chilies, sesame oil, soy sauce, Shaohsing wine, chili bean sauce, salt, and sugar.

Heat the peanut oil in a wok. When smoking add the asparagus and stir-fry for about 2 minutes, then add the stock. Reduce the liquid until thick but still slightly runny, then add the chili bean sauce mixture, mix, and heat for about 30 seconds. Add the noodles and lettuce, combine thoroughly with the sauce and heat through. Serve immediately.

v Stir-fried Noodles with Vegetables

Although I love all kinds of stir-fried noodles, this is one of my favourite versions, comprising fresh vegetables, mushrooms and a selection of delicious garnishes. Like many other recipes in this book it is entirely meatless. Serves two people as a complete meal, four as a starter.

225g/8oz dried egg noodles or
*   450g/1lb fresh egg 'oil' noodles*
3 tbsp peanut oil
2cm/3/4 inch piece of fresh ginger, peeled
*   and finely chopped*
3 cloves of garlic, peeled and thinly sliced
6 spring onions (scallions), sliced
1 stick (stalk) of celery, thinly sliced
1 red pepper, seeded, de-pithed and diced
100g/4oz oyster mushrooms, sliced or left
*   whole if small*
100g/4oz button mushrooms, sliced
1 whole egg and 1 egg yolk, beaten with a
*   pinch of salt*
2 tbsp soy sauce
1 tbsp tomato ketchup
100g/4oz fresh bean sprouts
1 lettuce heart or 'little gem' lettuce,
*   shredded*
2 tbsp cashews, coarsely chopped
small handful of fresh coriander (cilantro),
*   chopped*
1 tsp sugar
1/4–1/2 tsp cayenne
2 halved limes or 1 quartered lemon

Prepare the dried egg noodles by boiling according to the packet instructions or until *al dente*. Rinse in cold water and drain well. (Omit this step if you are using egg 'oil' noodles.)

Heat the oil in a wok. When smoking, add the ginger, garlic and spring onions. Mix once, then quickly add the celery and diced pepper. Stir-fry for 1 minute. Add the mushrooms and stir-fry for 2 minutes longer. Add the noodles and mix. Pour in the beaten egg, soy sauce, then add the tomato ketchup and bean sprouts. Mix thoroughly and stir-fry until heated through. Transfer the noodles on to a warmed, shallow serving dish. Surround them with the shredded lettuce and sprinkle the cashews, coriander, sugar and cayenne on top. Squeeze the lime or lemon juice over the noodles and serve straight away.

[v] Noodles with Acorn Squash, Tomatoes and Basil

I love to cook with fresh summer vegetables, as in this marriage of east and west. Despite the soy sauce, I imagine that the sauce would go equally well with Italian pasta. If you can get them, do use 'vine' tomatoes, which when ripe are very juicy and exceptionally flavourful. Ripe plum tomatoes will do well. Enough for two if you're very hungry, or serves four as an appetizer.

400g/14oz fresh egg or wheat noodles
3 tbsp peanut oil
2cm/3/4 inch piece of fresh ginger, peeled
    and finely chopped
2 fresh chilies, seeded and chopped
4 shallots, peeled and chopped
3 cloves of garlic, peeled and finely
    chopped
1 small acorn squash, peeled, de-seeded
    and finely diced
4 very ripe fresh vine or plum tomatoes,
    peeled and finely chopped
1 tsp sugar
1/2 tsp salt
juice of half a lemon
1 tbsp light soy sauce
1 tbsp dark soy sauce
small handful of fresh basil leaves,
    shredded

Boil the noodles in abundant water until *al dente*, rinse and drain. Heat the oil in a wok until smoking. Add the ginger, chilies, shallots and garlic and toss for 30 seconds. Add the diced acorn squash and toss for 1 minute longer. Add the tomatoes, sugar, salt, lemon juice, soy and fish sauces. Mix well and toss for 1 more minute or until thick. Add the noodles and basil, mix thoroughly and heat through. Turn on to a serving platter and eat straight away.

V Egg Noodles with Pattypan Squash

Pattypan are a tiny, thin-skinned variety of squash in season in the early summer. Small, young and firm courgettes may be substituted. Fresh egg ribbon noodles work best here. This recipe serves two people.

225g/8oz pattypan squash or young courgettes (zucchini)
350g/12oz fresh egg noodles
4 tbsp peanut oil
3 cloves of garlic, peeled and thinly sliced
1cm/½ inch cube fresh ginger, peeled and finely chopped
4 fresh chilies, seeded and thinly sliced
4 spring onions (scallions), washed, green and white sections separated, and sliced into thick chunks
120ml/4fl oz/½ cup chopped tomatoes (canned ones are fine)
1 tbsp light soy sauce
1 tbsp Shaohsing wine
salt and freshly ground black pepper
2-3 sprigs fresh mint, washed and chopped
1 tsp sugar
2 tbsp roasted peanuts, crushed

Wash, top and tail the pattypan squash, and cut them into small chunks. Bring a large pan of water to the boil, add the egg noodles, return to the boil and cook until *al dente*. Rinse and drain.

Heat the peanut oil in a wok until just smoking. Add the squash and stir-fry for 2 minutes. Add the garlic, ginger, chilies and white parts of the spring onions. Stir-fry for 2 minutes longer. Add the tomatoes, soy sauce and Shaohsing wine, season, and stir-fry for 3 minutes. Add the egg noodles and stir-fry for 1 minute more, to combine thoroughly with the sauce. Turn on to a warm serving platter and sprinkle with the green spring onion sections, the chopped mint, sugar and peanuts.

v Fried Egg Noodles with Water Chestnuts

I love the crunchy texture of water chestnuts which contrast well with the soft egg noodles. This recipe serves two to four people, depending upon how hungry they are!

350g/12oz dried egg noodles
4 tbsp peanut oil
1 red onion, peeled and finely chopped
1 carrot, peeled and very finely chopped
3 cloves of garlic, crushed, peeled and
*   sliced*
2cm/³/4 inch piece of fresh ginger, peeled
*   and finely chopped*
225g/8oz canned water chestnuts, drained
*   and sliced*
1 tsp sugar
¹/2 tsp salt
1 tbsp light soy sauce
2 tsp chili sauce
1 tbsp Shaohsing wine
2 tsp sesame oil
110g/4oz bean sprouts
2–3 fresh chilies, seeded and sliced
handful of fresh coriander (cilantro),
*   chopped*

Bring a large pan of water to the boil, add the noodles and boil as directed on the packet instructions or until *al dente*. Rinse and drain.

Heat the oil in a wok until smoking. Add the red onion and carrot and stir-fry for 2 minutes. Add the garlic, ginger, and water chestnuts and stir-fry for 2 minutes longer. Add the sugar, salt, soy sauce, chili sauce, Shaohsing wine and sesame oil. Mix well, then add the bean sprouts and the noodles. Stir-fry for about 2 minutes and serve on a warmed platter. Sprinkle with the chopped chilies and fresh coriander, and eat immediately.

Indonesian Stir-fried Noodles

As is usual in south-east Asian cooking, only a little meat is included, just enough to give some texture and flavour. This serves three to four people.

225g/8oz dried egg noodles
6 tbsp peanut oil
1 red onion, peeled and thinly sliced
2 cloves of garlic, peeled and thinly sliced
100g/4oz Chinese leaf cabbage, shredded
1 carrot, scrubbed and finely chopped
2 ripe tomatoes, chopped
white part of 4 spring onions (scallions),
*   thinly sliced*
2 fresh chilies, seeded and thinly sliced
1/4–1/2 tsp cayenne
100g/4oz cooked chicken meat, shredded
350ml/12fl oz/1 1/2 cups chicken
*   stock/broth (see page 50)*
2 tbsp light soy sauce
small handful of fresh coriander (cilantro),
*   washed and chopped*

Boil the noodles until *al dente* or according to the packet instructions, then rinse and drain thoroughly. Heat the oil to smoking point in a wok. Fry half the onion until browned and crisp but without burning. Drain on absorbent paper.

Discard all but 2–3 tbsp of the oil and re-heat what remains. Add the rest of the onion, the garlic and all the vegetables, including the spring onions and chilies. Toss in the oil for 30 seconds, then add the cayenne and the noodles and stir-fry for 1 minute. Add the chicken meat, the stock and soy sauce, stir and cook for 2 minutes longer. Turn into a serving bowl, sprinkle the fried onion and coriander on top and eat straight away.

Noodles with Oyster Mushrooms, Prawns and Alfalfa Sprouts

This is a delicious medley of flavours and textures, which also packs a lot of goodness. Other sprouted beans may be substituted should alfalfa be unavailable. Serves two to three people.

225g/8oz dried, thread egg noodles
1 large egg, beaten
4 tbsp peanut oil
2cm/3/4 inch piece of fresh ginger, peeled and finely chopped
2 fresh chilies, seeded and finely chopped
3 cloves of garlic, peeled and finely chopped
2 shallots, peeled and finely chopped
75g/3oz yellow or pink oyster mushrooms or very small grey oyster mushrooms, stems trimmed (tear large ones into chunks)
100g/4oz peeled cooked prawns (shrimp), thawed if frozen
1 tbsp Kikkoman's soy sauce plus extra to season
1 tbsp rice vinegar
1 tbsp dark sesame oil
50g/2oz alfalfa sprouts
3 tbsp cashew nuts, finely chopped or lightly crushed
generous handful of fresh coriander (cilantro), chopped

Boil the noodles until *al dente* or as directed on the packet instructions. Rinse and drain. Make an omelette with the beaten egg; do this in a small frying pan with a few drops of the oil and a pinch of salt. Cut into strips and set aside.

Heat the remaining peanut oil in a wok until just smoking. Add the ginger, chilies, garlic and shallots and stir-fry for 30 seconds. Add the oyster mushrooms and stir-fry for 1 minute. Add the prawns and stir-fry for 30 seconds longer. Add the noodles and stir-fry for 1 minute, taking care to combine all the ingredients thoroughly. Add the soy sauce, rice vinegar and sesame oil, combine thoroughly and heap on to a warmed serving platter. Scatter the alfalfa sprouts, the shredded omelette, chopped or crushed nuts, and coriander on top. Serve straight away with additional soy sauce, to taste.

Chow Mein

Chow Mein is the somewhat broad Chinese name for stir-fried noodles, usually containing some meat, fish or poultry although, albeit improperly, there is no reason why they should not also be vegetarian. Each of the following recipes will serve four people if combined with a small selection of Chinese dishes.

Beef Chow Mein

225g/8oz dried egg noodles
100g/4oz rump or sirloin steak (trimmed weight)
2 tsp dark soy sauce
3 tsp sesame oil
1 tsp plus 1 tbsp Shaohsing wine
1 tsp flour
1 tsp sugar
freshly ground black pepper
6 tbsp peanut oil
4 spring onions (scallions), thickly sliced, the white and green parts separated
3 cloves of garlic, peeled and finely chopped
2 fresh chilies, seeded and sliced
75g/3oz canned water chestnuts, rinsed, drained and chopped
50g/2oz Chinese leaf cabbage, shredded
2 tbsp light soy sauce

Boil the noodles until *al dente* or as directed on the packet. Rinse in cold running water, drain well and set aside.

Cut the beef into thin strips no bigger than 2cm/³/₄ inch long and 5mm/¹/₄ inch wide. Mix together in a bowl the dark soy sauce, 1 tsp sesame oil, 1 tsp Shaohsing wine, the flour, sugar and black pepper. Add the beef, stir around to coat thoroughly, then set aside for 30–60 minutes.

Heat the peanut oil to smoking point in a wok. Lift the beef from its marinade and deep-fry for 30 seconds. Remove with a slotted spoon and set aside. Remove all but about 2 tbsp of the oil. Re-heat and add the white part of the spring onion, the garlic, chilies and water chestnuts. Mix well, stir-fry for 2–3 minutes, then add the cabbage, return the beef and stir-fry for just 30 seconds. Add the noodles, toss to coat with the vegetables, then add the light soy sauce, 1 tbsp of the Shaohsing wine and the rest of the sesame oil. Toss until heated through, then turn on to a serving platter, scatter the green part of the spring onions on top and eat straight away.

· ·

Chicken Chow Mein

Substitute a skinned, boneless chicken breast for the beef. Cut it into similar-sized strips. Using just 2 tbsp oil do not deep-fry the chicken but instead, stir-fry it with the spring onion. Otherwise proceed as in the beef recipe.

Ham and Mushroom Chow Mein

225g/8oz dried egg noodles
3 tbsp peanut oil
100g/4oz button mushrooms, thinly sliced
3 ripe tomatoes, peeled and diced
white part of 4 spring onions (scallions),
*   thinly sliced*
2 cloves of garlic, peeled and finely
*   chopped*
50g/2oz frozen peas, thawed
50g/2oz cooked ham, diced
1 tsp sugar
1 tbsp Shaohsing wine
1 tbsp light soy sauce
2 tsp sesame oil

Boil the noodles until *al dente* or as directed on the packet. Rinse in cold running water, drain well and set aside.

Heat the oil to smoking point in a wok. Add the mushrooms and stir-fry for 1 minute, then add the tomatoes and stir-fry for 1 minute longer, add the spring onions, garlic, peas and ham, and stir-fry for 2–3 minutes, then add the sugar, Shaohsing wine and soy sauce and cook for 30 seconds longer. Add the noodles, toss to coat and heat through. Tip on to a serving platter, sprinkle the sesame oil on top and eat straight away.

Variation:
For a stronger flavour replace the cooked ham with an aged raw ham such as *prosciutto di Parma, jamon serrano* or Bayonne ham.

v Vegetable Chow Mein

This delicious recipe is suitable for vegetarians. Other combinations will work equally well, and exotic vegetables such as Chinese flowering cabbage, *pak choy* and water chestnuts are all exceptionally good stir-fried with noodles. Serves three people.

225g/8oz dried egg noodles
3 tbsp peanut oil
2 cloves of garlic, peeled and finely
    chopped
2cm/³/4 inch piece of fresh ginger, peeled
    and finely chopped
1 carrot, scrubbed and finely diced
2 celery sticks (stalks), thinly sliced
75g/3oz green beans, trimmed, cut in half
    and blanched
1 small green pepper, seeded, de-pithed
    and diced
1 fresh chili, seeded and thinly sliced
100g/4oz canned bamboo shoots, rinsed
    and thinly sliced
4 spring onions (scallions), sliced, the
    white and green parts separated
100g/4oz bean sprouts
1 tsp sugar
¹/2 tsp salt
1 tbsp Shaohsing wine
1 tbsp light soy sauce
1 tbsp dark soy sauce
1 tsp sesame oil

Boil the noodles until *al dente* or as directed on the packet. Rinse under cold water, drain well and set aside.

Heat the oil to smoking point in a wok. Add the garlic and ginger, stir, then add the carrot, celery, beans, green pepper and chili. Stir-fry for 1 minute, then add the bamboo shoots and the white part of the spring onions. Stir-fry for 2 minutes longer, then add the bean sprouts. Stir-fry for 30 seconds, then add the sugar, salt, Shaohsing wine, soy sauces, noodles, and toss together to coat and heat through. Tip on to a serving platter, sprinkle the sesame oil and green part of the spring onions on top, and eat straight away.

Variation:
Non-vegans may like to add a garnish of thin omelette strips made with a whole egg and an egg yolk, beaten.

v Vegetarian Yaki-Soba Noodles

A delicious, quick, vegetarian Japanese-style version of *Chow mein*. The fresh *yaki-soba* noodles, which resemble fresh spaghettini, are available from London's leading Japanese centre *Yao-han*, a retail complex that also operates a mail order service (see page 141 for details). The noodles come in a package that includes a dried sauce mix which, unfortunately, includes mono-sodium glutamate. For those with an aversion or allergy to this substance I have improvised an excellent home-made version. This is my adaptation of the standard *yaki-soba* recipe, which serves three people.

3 tbsp corn oil
1 small onion, peeled and finely chopped
2 cloves of garlic, peeled and finely
 chopped
2 celery sticks (stalks), thinly sliced
2 carrots, scrubbed and very thinly sliced
100g/4oz canned water chestnuts, rinsed,
 drained and sliced
175g/6oz bean sprouts
450g/1lb fresh yaki-soba or thin egg
 noodles
6 tbsp vegetable stock/broth (see page 51)
 or water (see note)
3 sachets ready-made yaki-soba sauce or
 the full quantity of sauce opposite

Heat the oil in a wok. When smoking add the onion and garlic and stir-fry for 30 seconds, then add the celery, carrots and water chestnuts. Stir-fry for 3 minutes, then add the bean sprouts. Mix, then add the noodles and the stock or water. Toss for 2 minutes, then add the sauce mixture and cook for 30 seconds. Eat straight away.

Note: If using the freshly made sauce reduce the stock or water to just 3 tbsp.

Variations:
2–4 shredded Chinese cabbage leaves, some sliced mushrooms and a seeded, de-pithed and diced green pepper may be added, but if so reduce the quantities of the other vegetables.

For a very good non-vegetarian version, reduce the quantities of the vegetables and add to the stir-fry base (at the step when the noodles are added): 100g/4oz cooked and shredded chicken, beef or pork, and 6–8 peeled, cooked prawns (shrimp). Proceed as above.

v My yaki-soba sauce

This makes enough to dress 450g/1lb fresh noodles.

3 tbsp Kikkoman's soy sauce
2 tsp corn oil
2 tsp rice vinegar
2 tsp mirin
2 tsp sugar
1/2 tsp salt
1/4 tsp cayenne
1/8 tsp Japanese 7-spice mixture
1 clove of garlic, peeled and crushed

Mix all the ingredients together in a cup, dissolving the sugar and salt, then leave for at least 30 minutes. When the noodles are nearly ready to eat, remove the garlic, stir the mixture, pour over the noodles and cook for 1 minute longer.

v Stir-fried Rice Noodles with Mushrooms and Aubergine

I created and tested this tasty and exotic vegetarian dish when I had a surplus supply of a wild fungus called *sparassis crispa*, which is similar to a Far Eastern species which the Chinese call 'silver ears'. That fungus is sold dried in Chinese supermarkets, but any fresh mushrooms (or dried and reconstituted ones) may be substituted. Serves two to three people.

225g/8oz thin rice noodles ('vermicelli')
1 small aubergine (eggplant)
110g/4oz fresh mushrooms, cleaned and
    sliced (or 25g/1oz dried mushrooms)
2 tsp sugar
1 tsp flour
2 tbsp light soy sauce
1 tbsp tomato ketchup
1 tsp rice vinegar
2 tsp chili sauce
4 tbsp water or stock (broth)
4 tbsp peanut oil
3 spring onions (scallions), peeled and
chopped, white and green parts
    separated
3 cloves of garlic, peeled and finely
    chopped
small piece of fresh galangal or ginger,
    peeled and finely chopped
1 stick (stalk) of lemon grass, trimmed and
    thinly sliced
2 fresh red chilies, seeded and chopped
2 tbsp cashews, chopped or lightly crushed

Bring a large pan of water to the boil, remove from the heat and add the 'vermicelli', leave for about 3 minutes or until tender, rinse and drain thoroughly.

Cut the aubergine into 1cm/½ inch cubes. Cut the fungus into small chunks of about 2cm/¾ inch; if using oyster, shiitake or button mushrooms just slice them. Dried mushrooms must be soaked in a cup of hot water for 20–30 minutes, rinsed and thinly sliced; remove the tough stalks if using dried shiitake mushrooms. In a cup or bowl mix together the sugar, flour, soy, tomato ketchup, rice vinegar, chili sauce and water or stock.

Heat 3 tbsp of the oil to smoking point in a wok, add the aubergines and stir-fry for 2 minutes. Add the rest of the oil, the white part of the spring onions, the garlic, *galangal* or ginger, and lemon grass, mix well and stir-fry for 1 minute longer. Add the mushrooms and stir-fry for 2 minutes. Pour in the sauce and, stirring constantly, cook until it starts to thicken (about 30 seconds). Add the 'vermicelli', toss to coat and eat straight away, garnished with the chillies, the green part of the spring onions and the cashews.

[v] Stir-fried Noodles with Mushrooms, Broccoli and Bean Sprouts

A delicious vegetarian stir-fry cooked in the Thai style. For this dish I much prefer the plump, soft texture of fresh egg 'oil' noodles but regular egg noodles, fresh or dried, will do very well. Serves two to three people.

450g/1lb fresh egg 'oil' noodles or 225g/8oz
  dried egg noodles
75g/3oz small broccoli florets plus their
  stalks
3 tbsp peanut oil
4 red shallots or 3 yellow shallots, peeled
  and chopped
3 cloves of garlic, peeled and chopped
1–4 small, dried hot red chilies, crumbled
  (preferably Thai birds'-eye chilies)
100g/4oz button mushrooms, quartered
2 tbsp light soy sauce
1 egg plus 1 egg yolk, beaten
75g/3oz bean sprouts
juice of 2 limes
50g/2oz roasted peanuts, crushed
handful of fresh coriander (cilantro),
  chopped
1/4–1/2 tsp cayenne
1 tsp sugar

Boil the noodles until *al dente* or according to the packet instructions, then, saving the cooking water, rinse and drain. (Omit this step if you are using fresh egg 'oil' noodles.)

Cut the stem part of the broccoli into chunks half the size of the florets: the florets themselves should be trimmed down to about 4cm/1½ inches at their widest and 5cm/2 inches in length. Return the cooking water to the boil, add a pinch of salt and immerse the broccoli, return to the boil and cook until vivid green but not quite *al dente* – about 3 minutes – then plunge into cold water and drain.

Heat the oil to smoking point in a wok. Add the shallots, garlic and chilies, stir-fry for a few seconds, then add the mushrooms and broccoli and cook for 2 minutes longer. Add the fish and soy sauces, mix once, then stir in the beaten egg and quickly add the noodles to the wok. Stir-fry for 1 minute, add the bean sprouts, turn to mix thoroughly, then transfer the wok contents on to a serving dish. Squeeze the lime over the noodles, scatter with the peanuts and coriander, and sprinkle the cayenne and sugar on top. Eat straight away.

Garlicky Fried-Egg Noodles with Vegetables

A delicious vegetable and noodle stir-fry with an agreeably hot and sour flavour, and with the unusual but wonderfully effective topping of fried eggs. Adjust the number of eggs and the amount of oil needed for frying them according to whether you are serving two or three people, for whom it will make a complete light meal or a substantial snack.

100g/4oz green beans
2 small courgettes (zucchini)
1 large carrot, scrubbed
4–5 tbsp peanut oil
4 cloves of garlic, peeled and thinly sliced
4 spring onions (scallions), sliced, the
    white and green parts separated
2 tsp chili sauce
6 tbsp vegetable stock/broth (see page 51)
    or water
1 tbsp light soy sauce
1 tbsp fish sauce (substitute dark soy if
    strictly for vegetarians)
450g/1lb fresh egg 'oil' noodles
2–3 eggs
10cm/4 inch section of cucumber, peeled
    and thinly sliced
50g/2oz roasted peanuts, lightly crushed
juice of 2 limes
1/2–1tsp cayenne
2 tsp sugar

Trim the green beans and chop them into 2cm/3/4 inch sections. Halve the courgettes from end to end and slice them into 5mm/1/4 inch thick half moon discs. Finely dice the carrot.

Heat 2 tbsp oil to smoking point in a wok, add the garlic, stir once, then add the green beans, courgettes, carrot and the white part of the spring onions. Stir-fry for 1 1/2 minutes, then add the chili sauce, stock or water, and the soy and fish sauces. Cook for about 3 minutes or until the sauce has reduced by half. Add the noodles, toss to coat with the vegetables and heat through, then transfer to a warmed serving dish. Cover loosely with foil to keep warm while you fry the eggs.

Heat 1 tbsp oil for each egg to be fried. When just smoking add the eggs and fry until done to your liking. Lift from the pan with a spatula and carefully place the eggs, without breaking the yolks, over the noodles. Surround the noodles with the cucumber slices. Scatter the peanuts and the green part of the spring onions on top, sprinkle with lime juice, cayenne and sugar, and eat straight away.

Noodles with Mussels and Black Beans

This excellent dish features the classic marriage of molluscs and aromatic black bean sauce. Clams would be the usual ingredient but as they can be hard to find I have substituted mussels.

225g/8oz dried kishimen noodles or other
  dried wheat noodles
675g/1¹/₂lb mussels
2 tbsp sesame oil
4 cloves of garlic, peeled and thinly sliced
2cm/³/₄ inch piece of fresh ginger, peeled
  and finely chopped
4 spring onions (scallions), coarsely
  chopped, the white and green parts
  separated
2 heaped tbsp black beans, rinsed, drained
  and chopped
1 tbsp Shaohsing wine
1 tbsp light soy sauce
2 tbsp dark soy sauce
7 tbsp water or fish stock (broth)
small handful of fresh coriander (cilantro),
  chopped

Bring a large pan of water to the boil, add the noodles, return to the boil and cook until *al dente*, then rinse under cold water and drain thoroughly. Meanwhile, sort the mussels, discarding any that are not tightly closed or any that are cracked. Scrub and wash them in several changes of fresh water and remove any fibre and beard.

Heat the sesame oil to smoking point in a wok and stir-fry the garlic, ginger and the white part of the spring onion for 30 seconds, then add the black beans. Stir and pour in the Shaohsing wine, stir again, then add the light and dark soy sauces, the water or stock, and the mussels. Cover the wok, reduce the heat, and cook for 15 minutes. With a slotted spoon, remove the mussels, leaving the other ingredients behind in the wok, which should be taken off the heat. The shells should have opened; discard any that haven't. Remove the meats from their shells, discard the shells and put the meats back into the wok. Add the noodles and heat through, turning to coat with the ingredients.

Transfer on to a warmed serving platter, scatter the coriander and the green part of the spring onions on top, and serve immediately.

Stir-fried Noodles with Crab

A fairly simple dish which I have adapted from the late Jeremy Round's recipe in *The Independent Cook* (Barrie & Jenkins, 1988). The strong-tasting crab meat must be very, very fresh or it will taste unpleasantly fishy. Serves two to three people.

175g/6oz thin, dried egg noodles
100g/4oz aubergine/eggplant (trimmed weight)
3 tbsp peanut oil
8 small red or 4 yellow shallots, peeled and sliced
2cm/3/4 inch piece of fresh ginger, peeled and finely chopped
1–2 fresh chilies, seeded and finely chopped
4 spring onions (scallions), coarsely chopped, the white and green parts separated
1 heaped tbsp tomato ketchup
1 tbsp Shaohsing wine
100g/4oz fresh crab meat
1 tbsp light soy sauce
2 tsp chili sauce
2 tsp rice vinegar
juice of 1/2 lemon

Bring a large pan of water to the boil, add the noodles, return to the boil and, stirring to separate the strands, cook until *al dente*. Rinse under cold water and drain. Cut the aubergine into thumbnail-size cubes.

Heat the oil to smoking point in a wok. Fry the shallots, ginger and chilies for a few seconds, then add the white part of the spring onions, the ketchup and aubergine, and stir-fry for 1 minute longer. Pour in the Shaohsing wine, cover the wok and cook gently for 2 minutes or until the aubergine is just tender, stirring once or twice to prevent burning. Add the crab meat and stir-fry for 1 minute longer, then add the soy and chili sauces, and the vinegar. Stir, add the noodles and toss to coat.

As soon as the noodles are hot transfer the wok contents to a serving platter, squeeze the lemon juice on top and scatter over the green part of the spring onions. Eat straight away.

Fresh Udon Noodles with Prawns and Green Beans

I love the fat shape and soft texture of
fresh *udon* noodles which will be found in
Japanese shops and some Chinese supermarkets. However, this recipe owes more
to lip-smacking Thai and south-east Asian
influences than to the land of the rising
sun. Serves three to four people.

*100g/4oz green or yardlong beans,
trimmed and cut into 2cm/3/4 inch
    sections*
450g/1lb fresh udon noodles
*100g/4oz raw or cooked prawns (shrimp),
    thawed if frozen*
3 tbsp peanut oil
*3 cloves of garlic, peeled and finely
    chopped*
1 red onion, peeled and chopped
1 egg plus 1 egg yolk, beaten
1 tbsp light soy sauce
1 tbsp hoisin sauce
1 tsp sugar
6 tbsp chicken stock/broth (see page 50)
100g/4oz bean sprouts
*7.5cm/3 inch section of cucumber, peeled
    and thinly sliced*
50g/2oz roasted peanuts, lightly crushed
1/4–1/2 tsp chili flakes or cayenne
1 lime, quartered
*1/8–1/4 tsp Japanese 7-spice mixture
    (optional)*

Blanch the beans in a large pan of boiling
salted water for just 1 minute, remove with
a slotted spoon, plunge into cold water
and drain. Bring the water back to the
boil, add the noodles, return to the boil
and cook for 30 seconds, then rinse under
cold water and drain. Peel the raw prawns.

Heat the oil to smoking point in a wok,
add the garlic and onion and stir-fry for
1 minute. Add the raw prawns, beans, egg,
soy and hoisin sauces, sugar, and stir for 1
minute. Add the noodles, the cooked
prawns, if relevant, the stock and half the
bean sprouts, mix well and continue to
cook for 1 1/2 minutes longer. Tip the wok
contents on to a serving platter, surround
the noodles with the remaining bean
sprouts and the cucumber, sprinkle with
the peanuts and chili flakes or cayenne,
and squeeze a little lime juice over the
noodles. If you want extra pep, sprinkle
the 7-spice mixture on top. Eat straight
away.

Fried Rice Noodles with Tiger Prawns and Vegetables

A delicious Thai-style recipe which is shown on the front cover of the book. Do not be put off by the long list of ingredients since their preparation and cooking can all be accomplished within half an hour, and I have done it in less than 20 minutes!

Fat, juicy tiger prawns which are now stocked by the leading supermarkets, and sweet, lightly cooked vegetables flavour the bland, slightly sticky noodles.

If you can get them, do substitute raw, unshelled tiger prawns, which should be peeled and briefly fried first until just pink, then added to the wok together with the drained noodles. Serves two people as a complete meal; four to six as an appetizer or accompanied by other dishes.

175g/6oz thin rice noodles ('vermicelli')
4 tbsp peanut oil
1–2 large, dried red chili peppers, coarsely chopped
2cm/3/4 inch piece of fresh ginger, peeled and finely chopped
3 cloves of garlic, peeled and finely chopped
4 spring onions (scallions), sliced, white and green parts separated
1 stick (stalk) of celery, thinly sliced
1/2 sweet red pepper, seeded, de-pithed and diced
75g/3oz oyster mushrooms, sliced or left whole if small
50g/2oz fresh shiitake mushrooms, sliced
100g/4oz peeled, cooked tiger prawns (shrimp), halved if very large, thawed if frozen
1 whole egg and 1 egg yolk, beaten
1 tbsp soy sauce
1 tbsp Thai fish sauce
1 tbsp tomato ketchup
juice of 1 lime
100g/4oz fresh bean sprouts
1 'little gem' lettuce, shredded
2 tbsp roasted peanuts, lightly pounded
1 tsp sugar
small handful of fresh coriander (cilantro), chopped

Bring a large pan of water to the boil, add the noodles, stir, remove from the heat and leave to soak for 3–4 minutes or until tender. Rinse in cold water and drain well and, unless you intend to proceed without delay, toss the noodles in 1 tbsp of the oil to prevent them from sticking together.

Heat the remaining oil in a wok. When smoking, add the dried red chili and fry until dark but not burnt black, which can happen in seconds. Remove the chili and reserve. Add the ginger, garlic and the white part of the spring onions to the wok,

mix once, then add the celery and diced red pepper. Stir-fry for 1 minute. Add the mushrooms and stir-fry for 3 minutes longer. Add the cooked prawns and the noodles and mix. Pour in the beaten egg, the soy and fish sauces, the tomato ketchup and lime juice. Mix well and add the bean sprouts, shredded lettuce, and peanuts. Mix again and transfer immediately to a serving dish. Sprinkle the sugar, coriander, fried chili pieces and the green part of the spring onions on top. Eat straight away.

Fresh 'Oil' Noodles with Allspice-Chicken and Red Pepper

The success of this quick, simple dish depends upon the quality of the noodles, and you will have to go to a Chinese supermarket to buy the shiny, yellow, fresh egg 'oil' noodles. Serves two to three people.

1 chicken breast fillet, skinned
salt and freshly ground black pepper
1/2 tsp ground allspice
1 egg white, lightly beaten with a fork
2 tsp Shaohsing wine
2 tsp sesame oil
2 tbsp peanut oil
3 cloves of garlic, peeled and thinly sliced
1 small red pepper, seeded, de-pithed and
    diced
2 tbsp tomato ketchup
1 tbsp light soy sauce
100g/4oz bean sprouts
450g/1lb fresh egg 'oil' noodles
3 spring onions (scallions), thinly sliced
50g/2oz roasted peanuts, lightly crushed
1/2–1 tsp chili flakes or to taste

Cut the chicken breast into small, bite-size cubes. Put them in a bowl, then add the seasoning, allspice, egg white, Shaohsing wine and sesame oil. Stir to coat, cover the bowl and set aside for 30 minutes.

Heat the peanut oil to smoking point in a wok, then add the garlic and toss for a few seconds. Remove from the heat. Lift the chicken strips from the marinade with a slotted spoon, drain briefly, then return the wok to the heat, add the chicken and stir-fry for 2 minutes or until it turns white. Add the diced red pepper, ketchup and soy sauce and continue to stir-fry for 1 minute longer. Add the bean sprouts and noodles, toss to heat through, turn on to a serving platter and sprinkle the spring onions, peanuts and chili flakes on top. Eat straight away

Noodles with Chicken in Hoisin Sauce

Hoisin sauce is made from soya beans, sugar, vinegar and garlic, and some brands go by the label 'barbecue sauce'. Combined with chicken it makes a delicious, glossy sauce for noodles. Serves two to three people.

1 large chicken breast, skinned and sliced
*   into small, thin strips*
1 tsp sesame oil
3 tsp light soy sauce
4 tsp Shaohsing wine
salt and freshly ground black pepper
225g/8oz thick or medium, dried egg
*   noodles*
3 tbsp peanut oil
4 cloves of garlic, peeled and thinly sliced
*   at a diagonal angle*
3 spring onions (scallions), coarsely sliced,
*   the white and green parts separated*
1 carrot, scrubbed and thinly sliced at a
*   diagonal angle*
1 celery stick (stalk), thinly sliced at a
*   diagonal angle*
2 tbsp hoisin sauce
6 tbsp water
50g/2oz roasted cashews

Combine in a bowl the chicken, sesame oil, 1 tsp light soy sauce and 2 tsp Shaohsing wine. Season with salt and pepper, mix and leave to marinate for 30 minutes. After about 20 minutes boil the egg noodles in abundant water until *al dente*, rinse under cold water and drain.

Heat the peanut oil to smoking point in a wok, add the garlic, the white part of the spring onions, carrots and celery and stir-fry for 2 minutes. Lift the chicken out of the marinade and add to the wok (reserving the marinade). Stir-fry until the chicken turns white, then add the remaining 2 tsp Shaohsing wine and 2 tsp light soy sauce. Stir, add the hoisin sauce, the marinade, water and cashews. Mix and add the noodles. Toss to coat and heat through, transfer to a warmed serving dish, scatter the green part of the spring onions over the noodles and serve immediately.

Noodles with Chicken and Mango

In this delicious dish the noodles are coated in a wonderful velvety mango sauce; and the sliced mango strips and green spring onions make an attractive, colourful garnish. This serves two or three people.

1 ripe mango, peeled
4 tsp Shaohsing wine
2 tsp light soy sauce
1/2 tsp turmeric
3 tbsp peanut oil
salt and freshly ground black pepper
1 large corn-fed chicken breast, skinned
   and thinly sliced
1 tbsp oyster sauce
2 tsp dark soy sauce
2 tbsp water
225g/8oz medium, dried egg noodles
2 dried, hot red chilies, chopped
4 spring onions (scallions), sliced, the
   white and green parts separated
3 cloves garlic, peeled and finely chopped

Dice approximately two thirds of the mango, mash to a pulp with a fork and put in a bowl. Slice the rest of the mango into thin strips and reserve. Add to the bowl 2 tsp Shaohsing wine, the light soy sauce, turmeric, 2 tsp of the oil, salt and pepper to taste, and the chicken. Mix well, cover and leave for at least 1 hour. Meanwhile mix together the oyster and dark soy sauces, and the water. About 10 minutes before you start the cooking boil the noodles until *al dente*, rinse under cold water and drain.

Heat the remaining oil in a wok until smoking. Add the dried chilies, the white part of the spring onions, the garlic, and stir once. Lift the chicken from the marinade with a slotted spoon and add it to the wok. Stir-fry for 2 minutes, then add the remaining marinade and stir-fry for about another 2 minutes or until much of the liquid has evaporated. Add the remaining Shaohsing wine, toss for 30 seconds, then add the oyster sauce mixture and continue to cook until it thickens – about 1 minute longer. Add the noodles to the wok, toss to coat, and heat through.

Transfer to a warmed serving platter, garnish with the green spring onion and the mango slices, and serve immediately.

Vietnamese-style Noodles with Lettuce and Mint

Here, fresh 'oil' noodles are the base for a delicious medley of hot, sweet, salty, sour and nutty flavours which characterize much Vietnamese cooking. The contrast of soft and crunchy textures is marvellous, and I count this among my favourite noodle recipes. Serves two to four people.

4 tbsp peanut oil
1 egg, beaten
1 carrot, scrubbed and diced
1 small red pepper, seeded, de-pithed and
*   diced*
2 cloves of garlic, peeled and finely
*   chopped*
2 fresh chilies, finely chopped
4 spring onions (scallions), sliced, the
*   green and white parts separated*
75g/3oz bean sprouts
4 Cos (romaine) lettuce leaves, cut into
*   2.5cm/1 inch sections, the green and*
*   white parts separated*
450g/1lb fresh 'oil' noodles
3 tsp sugar
juice of 2 limes or 1 lemon
75g/3oz shelled, cooked prawns (shrimp),
*   thawed if frozen*
2 tbsp fish sauce
2 tbsp soy sauce
5cm/2 inch section of cucumber, thinly
*   sliced*
1/2 tsp cayenne
small handful of fresh mint, chopped
50g/2oz roasted peanuts, lightly crushed

Heat 1 tbsp peanut oil in a wok until smoking. Add the beaten egg and make a small omelette. Remove, slice into strips and set aside.

Heat the rest of the oil until smoking. Add the carrot, red pepper, garlic, chilies and the white part of the spring onions and stir fry for about a minute. Add the bean sprouts and the white part of the lettuce and stir-fry for 30 seconds longer. Add the noodles, sugar, lime or lemon juice, prawns, fish and soy sauces and toss until thoroughly heated through. Turn on to a heated serving platter, surround with the green part of the lettuce and the cucumber, scatter the sliced omelette on top and sprinkle with cayenne, mint, green parts of the spring onion and peanuts. Serve straight away.

Singapore Fried Noodles

I had my first taste of noodles at the tender age of six. My father, who worked for Shell's Singapore office, loved buying tempting snacks from Chinese and Malay street vendors and, although at that time a very fussy little boy, I do recall being persuaded to try noodles, and liking them! There are countless variations on this dish, which may or may not include curry spices (see the recipe on page 137), but usually, rice noodles are the base. In fact the term 'Singapore noodles' is perhaps the least precise of all recipe titles in the noodles lexicon!

225g/8oz thin rice noodles ('vermicelli')
6 tbsp peanut oil
75g/3oz lean cooked ham, cut into small,
    thin strips
100g/4oz raw or cooked prawns (shrimp),
    peeled, and thawed if frozen
75g/3oz button mushrooms, thinly sliced
6 red or 4 yellow shallots, peeled and
    chopped
3 cloves of garlic, peeled and finely
    chopped
2.5cm/1 inch piece of fresh ginger, peeled
    and finely chopped
4 spring onions (scallions), sliced
1 tbsp chili sauce
3 tbsp chicken stock/broth (see page 50)
    or water
1/2 tsp sugar
1 tbsp light soy sauce
1 tbsp dark soy sauce
100g/4oz fresh bean sprouts

Bring abundant water to the boil, add the rice noodles, stir, then turn off the heat and let the noodles sit in the water for 5 minutes or until *al dente*. Rinse thoroughly in cold water and drain.

Heat the oil to smoking point in a wok. Add the ham and stir-fry for 1 minute. Lift with a slotted spoon and drain on absorbent paper. Add the raw prawns to the wok and stir-fry for 1 minute, then lift and drain on absorbent paper. (Cooked prawns should just go into the oil for 15 seconds to flavour the oil, then be removed and drained.)

Pour off half, and re-heat the remaining oil. Add the mushrooms, stir for 1 minute, then add the shallots, garlic and ginger and stir-fry for 30 seconds longer. Add the spring onions, chili sauce, stock or water, and sugar. Stir, then pour in the soy sauces, return the ham and prawns, add the noodles and bean sprouts and toss repeatedly to coat and heat the noodles through. When thoroughly hot turn on to a serving platter and eat straight away.

Pad Thai
(Thai fried rice noodles)

Thailand's most popular noodle dish usually replaces the ubiquitous plain boiled rice and accompanies other dishes of meat, poultry, fish and vegetables. Thai recipes specify the inclusion of dried prawns, but my preference is for fresh or frozen ones, which lack the hard crunch that is meant to contribute to the noodles' texture. The best noodles for this dish are Thai *sen lek*, which are thin, flat ribbon noodles made of rice flour requiring only a good soak in water without pre-boiling to soften them; Chinese 'rice vermicelli' may be substituted. This serves four (two if served as a complete meal).

225g/8oz thin, dried rice noodles
4 tbsp peanut oil
4 small, dried red chilies (preferably Thai birds'-eye chilies), crumbled
3 cloves of garlic, peeled and finely chopped
4 spring onions (scallions), thickly sliced, the white and green parts separated
1 egg, lightly beaten
juice of half a lemon
1¹/₂ tbsp tomato ketchup
1 tbsp fish sauce
1 tsp sugar
75g/3oz small peeled, cooked prawns (shrimp), thawed if frozen
50g/2oz fresh bean sprouts
2 tbsp roasted peanuts, crushed
small handful of fresh coriander (cilantro), chopped
¹/₄–¹/₂ tsp cayenne

Soak the noodles in plenty of cold water; they should soften after 20–30 minutes. Drain.

Heat the oil to smoking point in a wok. Add the chilies, garlic and the white part of the spring onions. Toss for 30 seconds, then add the beaten egg, lemon juice, ketchup, fish sauce and sugar. Stir for 20 seconds, then add the noodles, prawns and half the bean sprouts. Mix thoroughly and stir-fry the noodles for about a minute or until properly heated through. Turn on to a serving platter, scatter the remaining bean sprouts on top and sprinkle with the peanuts, coriander, green parts of the spring onions and cayenne, to taste. Serve straight away.

Mee Krob

(Crisp, deep-fried thin rice noodles)

No noodle recipe collection would be complete without this festive Thai dish. Very thin, dried rice noodles are deep-fried, becoming crisp and puffy in an instant in the boiling hot oil. Then they are combined with meat and/or poultry, prawns, beaten eggs and bathed in a hot, sweet and sour sauce. Fresh chilies, bean sprouts, and pickled garlic (see opposite) are among the many appropriate garnishes. There are many variations, some very elaborate, but my version is relatively straightforward. Breaking up the 'vermicelli' is messy as the shards are catapulted about but they can be contained inside a bag.

peanut or corn oil for deep frying
175g/6oz thin rice noodles ('vermicelli')
100g/4oz lean minced (ground) pork
100g/4oz skinned chicken breast, skinned and sliced into very small, thin strips
75g/3oz raw or cooked, peeled tiger prawns (shrimp), thawed if frozen
4 cloves of garlic, peeled and thinly sliced
1 red onion, peeled and chopped
1 tsp chili flakes
3 tbsp sugar
juice of 3 limes
1 tbsp fish sauce
1 tbsp light soy sauce
6 tbsp chicken stock/broth (see page 50)
2 eggs, beaten
2–4 fresh chilies, seeded and thinly sliced
100g/4oz bean sprouts
4–6 sliced cloves of pickled garlic (optional)
small handful of fresh coriander (cilantro), chopped

v Pickled Garlic

Heat a deep layer of oil in a wok until quite a lot of smoke rises. Meanwhile, put the noodles in a bag and pull them apart into clumps. Test a few strands before deep-frying the clumps: if they immediately crackle and swell, the oil has reached the right temperature. Add the noodle clumps to the wok in batches, and fry until well puffed and a light golden colour, turning each batch once, then remove with a large wire strainer or slotted spoon and drain on absorbent paper. When all the clumps have been deep-fried, place them on a very large serving dish and keep them warm in a cool oven while you prepare the rest of the dish.

Clean the wok and heat 3 tbsp oil to smoking point. Stir-fry for 30 seconds in succession: the pork, the chicken and the raw prawns (save cooked prawns for a later step). Now add the garlic, onion, and chili flakes, stir-fry for 2 minutes, then pour in the sugar, lime juice, fish sauce and stock. Stir until two thirds of the liquid has evaporated. If you are using cooked prawns add them to the wok now. Make a hole in the centre of the wok and pour in the beaten egg, stirring all the while. Before it sets completely, crumble the fried 'vermicelli' into the wok, stirring to combine as thoroughly as possible with the sauce. Turn on to a serving platter, scatter the fresh chilies, bean sprouts, pickled garlic slices and coriander over the noodles, and eat warm.

This recipe is adapted from Vatcharin Bhumichitr's *The Taste of Thailand* (Pavilion, 1988).

6 tsp sugar
2 tsp salt
250ml/8fl oz/1 cup rice or white wine
  vinegar
the peeled cloves from 2 heads of garlic

(Makes enough to fill a small jam jar.) In a small stainless steel, aluminium or enamelled pan, dissolve the sugar and salt in the vinegar over a high heat. When boiling fast, add the garlic cloves and return to the boil. Boil for 1 minute, then put the garlic cloves into a sterilised glass jar, pour the vinegar over them and seal when cool. Keep for 2 weeks before opening, and use up within 2 months.

Fried Noodle 'Cake' with Aromatic Chicken in Black Bean Sauce

Here, egg noodles are fried on both sides until crisp and golden-brown on the outside but with a soft centre; they are then served topped with chicken and green pepper in an aromatic black bean sauce. The fried noodle 'cake' is based on a recipe in Yan-kit So's *Classic Chinese Cookbook* (Dorling Kindersley, 1984), but the delectable topping that goes so well with it is my own. Serves two to three people.

2 small, boned, skinless chicken breasts,
    sliced into thin strips
1 tbsp light soy sauce
1 tbsp dark soy sauce
1 tbsp Shaohsing wine
2 tsp rice vinegar
freshly ground black pepper
175g/6oz dried egg noodles
110ml/4fl oz/½ cup peanut oil
4 cloves of garlic, peeled and thinly sliced
4 spring onions (scallions), trimmed and
    thickly sliced, the white and green parts
    separated
1 green pepper, seeded, de-pithed and
    diced
2 heaped tbsp fermented black beans,
    washed, drained and chopped
2 tsp chili sauce
6 tbsp chicken stock/broth (see page 50)
2 tsp sesame oil

Put the chicken in a bowl, add 2 tsp of each of the soy sauces, 2 tsp Shaohsing wine, and the rice vinegar. Season with freshly ground black pepper, combine thoroughly and set aside for 30 minutes to 2 hours. Meanwhile bring abundant water to the boil, add the noodles, separate the strands and cook until *al dente*, then rinse under cold water, drain very thoroughly, and pat dry with absorbent paper to remove all traces of moisture.

Heat 7 tbsp of the oil to smoking point in a wok, add the noodles and press them down with a spatula to make a thick layer. Fry until the base is golden-brown but not burnt, then loosen, turn and fry the other side until golden-brown.

Remove the noodle 'cake' with a spatula, scrape away any debris and wipe the wok clean. Keep the noodles warm on a serving platter lined with absorbent paper, which should be removed once the noodles are well-drained.

Re-heat the wok, add the remaining 1 tbsp oil and, when smoking, the garlic, the white part of the spring onions and the green pepper. Stir-fry for 1 minute, then lift the chicken from the marinade with a slotted spoon, drain, and add it to the wok, toss for 1½ minutes, then add the black beans, the remaining soy sauces and Shaohsing wine, the chili sauce and the stock. Toss for about 1½ minutes longer or until the chicken is cooked, then pour the wok contents over the noodle cake, sprinkle with the green part of the spring onions and the sesame oil, and eat immediately.

Fried Noodle 'Cake' with Sweet and Sour Chicken

Fried egg noodles make a crisp base with a soft centre, and have an entirely different texture to the deep-fried rice noodles on pages 104 and 108. Sweet and sour chicken makes a rich and luscious topping. Serves two to three people.

175g/6oz dried egg noodles
2 skinless, boned chicken breasts, cut into
  small, thin strips
3 tbsp dark soy sauce
1 tbsp Shaohsing wine
1 tsp sesame oil
salt and freshly ground pepper
100g/4oz fresh pineapple (peeled weight)
1 carrot, scrubbed
1 green pepper
white part of 6 spring onions (scallions)
1 tbsp sugar
2 tsp flour
3 tbsp rice vinegar
6 tbsp water
1 tbsp tomato ketchup
2 tbsp light soy sauce
120ml/4fl oz/1/2 cup peanut oil
3 cloves of garlic, peeled and thinly sliced

Bring a large pan of water to the boil, add the noodles, return to the boil and, separating the strands, cook until *al dente*, then rinse under cold water and leave to drain.

Put the chicken in a bowl, add the dark soy sauce, Shaohsing wine and sesame oil, season, cover and set aside. Cut the pineapple into small chunks. Slice the carrot at a diagonal angle into very thin oval discs. Remove the cap, pith and seeds of the green pepper and coarsely chop the flesh. Cut the spring onions into 2cm/3/4 inch sections.

Combine the sugar, flour, vinegar, water, ketchup and light soy sauce, stirring thoroughly to ensure that no lumps of flour remain. Set aside.

Heat the oil to smoking point in a wok, add the noodles and press them down with a spatula to make a thick layer. Fry until the base is golden-brown in patches but not burnt, then loosen, turn the 'cake' and fry the other side until similarly golden-brown. Remove the noodle 'cake' with a spatula and keep warm on a serving platter lined with absorbent paper.

Remove the chicken pieces from the marinade with a slotted spoon and drain, reserving the marinade. Re-heat the wok to smoking point (add more oil if necessary), add the chicken and toss until pale golden all over, then add the garlic and stir-fry for 30 seconds longer. Add the marinade, stir, then put in the pineapple chunks and all the other vegetables. Toss for 1 minute, then stir the sweet and sour sauce mixture, pour it into the wok, and continue to stir until the liquid has thickened (about 3 minutes longer). Pour over the noodles and eat straight away.

Crisp, Deep-Fried Noodles with Sweet and Sour Pork

Similar to the 'Fried noodles with sweet and sour chicken' (page 107), this dish is successful by virtue of the contrasts of textures and flavours. You will need two woks, or one wok and a large, lidded saucepan. This serves four people, preferably accompanied by a few other Oriental dishes.

225g/8oz pork loin or fillet, trimmed of fat
100g/4oz fresh, peeled (or canned)
  pineapple
1 large carrot, scrubbed
1 green pepper
4 spring onions (scallions)
flour for dusting the pork plus 1 tsp
2 tbsp water
1 tbsp sugar
3 tbsp rice vinegar
4 tbsp water
1 tbsp tomato ketchup
2 tbsp light soy sauce
peanut oil for deep-frying plus 3 tbsp
3 cloves of garlic, peeled and thinly sliced
2 tbsp Shaohsing wine
175g/6oz thin rice noodles ('vermicelli')

Cut the pork into 2cm/3/4 inch cubes. Cut the pineapple into similar-sized chunks. Slice the carrot at a slight diagonal angle into very thin, oval discs. Remove the cap, pith and seeds of the green pepper and coarsely chop the flesh. Cut the spring onions into 1cm/1/2 inch sections, separating the white and green parts.

Dissolve 1 tsp flour in 2 tbsp water and set aside. Mix the sugar, vinegar, water, ketchup, and soy sauce, stirring thoroughly to dissolve the sugar granules.

Dust the pork with a little flour. Heat 3 tbsp oil to smoking point in a wok or large saucepan, add the pork and toss in the oil for 2 minutes to seal on all sides, then add the garlic and stir-fry for 30 seconds longer. Add the Shaohsing wine, stir, then put in the pineapple chunks and all the vegetables except for the green part of the spring onions. Toss for 30 seconds, pour in the sweet and sour sauce and the flour mixture, and continue to stir until the liquid has thickened (3–5 minutes longer). Sprinkle with the green part of the spring onions, cover and keep warm while you deep-fry the noodles.

Heat a deep layer of oil in a wok until quite a lot of smoke rises. Meanwhile, break up the rice 'vermicelli' in a bag to contain the shards. Add the noodles to the wok in batches, and fry until puffed and light golden, turning each batch once, then remove with a large strainer or slotted spoon and drain on absorbent paper. Keep warm in a cool oven with the door ajar.

When all the 'vermicelli' has been fried divide into equal serving portions on warmed plates. Re-heat the sweet and sour pork and quickly serve over the noodles before they lose their crispness. Eat straight away.

Noodles with Minced Pork in Bean Sauce

A typical noodle dish from Northern China, this recipe is robust, uncomplicated and very tasty. Serves two to three people.

225g/8oz fresh egg ribbon noodles
2 tbsp peanut oil
4 cloves of garlic, peeled and finely
  chopped
2cm/³/4 inch piece of fresh ginger, peeled
  and finely chopped
4 spring onions (scallions), thinly sliced,
  white and green parts separated
1 tsp chili flakes
225g/8oz lean, minced pork
1–2 tsp sugar
3 tsp yellow bean sauce
3 tsp hoisin sauce
2 tbsp light soy sauce
120ml/4fl oz/¹/2 cup chicken stock/broth
  (see page 50)
2 tsp sesame oil
6cm/2¹/2 inch piece of cucumber, peeled
  and cut into matchstick pieces

Bring a large pan of water to the boil, add the noodles, return to the boil and cook for 1–2 minutes or until just *al dente*, then rinse and drain.

Heat the oil to smoking point in a wok, then add the garlic, ginger, and the white part of the spring onions. Stir a few times, then add the chili flakes and the pork. Breaking up the lumps, stir-fry for 2–3 minutes or until the meat is no longer raw-looking. Add the sugar, the yellow bean, hoisin and soy sauces, and the chicken stock. Cook for 1 minute, stirring constantly, then add the noodles and toss to coat; heat through, then turn on to a serving platter. Sprinkle with the sesame oil, and garnish with the green part of the spring onions and the cucumber strips. Eat straight away.

Wheat Noodles with Smoked Bacon, Broccoli and Sesame Seeds

For this delicious, quick noodle stir-fry I use any thick, fresh, round Japanese or Chinese wheat noodles; white, egg-less 'oil' noodles are ideal, but you will have to go to a Chinese supermarket to find them. They need no pre-boiling, and with their wonderful soft, bouncy texture they will more than repay the effort of tracking them down.

3 tsp sesame seeds
450g/1lb fresh, thick, round wheat noodles
175g/6oz broccoli, divided into bite-size small florets, including some small chunks cut from the upper stem
1 large carrot, scrubbed and diagonally sliced
3 tbsp corn oil
75g/3oz smoked back bacon, cut into large dice
2 cloves of garlic, peeled and finely chopped
2cm/3/4 inch piece of fresh ginger, peeled and finely chopped
white part of 4 spring onions (scallions), sliced
1 tbsp mirin
2 tbsp Kikkoman's soy sauce
2 tsp sesame oil

Toast the sesame seeds in a hot, dry pan until they start to jump. Remove and reserve. Bring abundant water to the boil. Add the noodles, return to the boil and cook for 30 seconds, then, saving the cooking water, rinse them in cold water and drain. (Omit this step if you are using Chinese 'oil' noodles.) Return the water to the boil and immerse the broccoli and carrots for 1 minute, then refresh in cold water and drain.

Heat the corn oil to smoking point in a wok. Add the bacon and stir-fry until nearly crisp, then add the garlic, ginger, broccoli and carrots. Stir-fry for 1 minute, add the spring onions and toss for 1 minute longer. Add the *mirin*, cook for 15 seconds, then add the noodles and soy sauce and toss until thoroughly coated and heated through.

Turn on to a serving platter, sprinkle the toasted sesame seeds and sesame oil on top and eat straight away.

Wheat Noodles with Beef, Green Pepper and Asparagus

You can use Japanese *somen* or *udon* noodles here, or indeed the more commonly available Chinese dried egg noodles. They make a delicious yet simple dish that is perfect for a nutritious light lunch or supper for two people; served as an appetizer it makes enough for four.

225g/8oz dried noodles
100g/4oz sirloin or rump steak, (trimmed weight)
1/2 tsp sugar
3 tsp mirin
2 tbsp Kikkoman's soy sauce
1 tbsp sesame oil
3 cloves of garlic, peeled and thinly sliced
small piece of fresh ginger, peeled and very finely chopped
2 fresh chilies, seeded and thinly sliced
4 spring onions (scallions), sliced into large chunks, the white and green parts separated
2 tbsp corn oil
1 green pepper, seeded, de-pithed and diced
100g/4oz thin asparagus, trimmed and cut into 2cm/3/4 inch sections
1/2 tsp salt

Bring a large pan of water to the boil. Immerse the noodles and boil until *al dente*. Rinse under cold running water, drain well and set aside.

Slice the beef into thin strips about 5mm/1/4 inch wide and 2cm/3/4 inch long. Combine the beef in a bowl with the sugar, *mirin*, 1 tbsp soy sauce, 2 tsp sesame oil, garlic, ginger, chilies, and the white part of the spring onions. Cover and set aside for 20 minutes.

Heat the corn oil in a wok until smoking. Add the green pepper and asparagus and stir-fry for 1 minute. Season with salt. Tip the beef and its marinade into the wok and toss for 2–3 minutes longer or until the beef and vegetables are cooked through. Add the noodles, the remaining sesame oil and soy sauce. Stir-fry until heated through and transfer the wok contents on to a serving platter. Sprinkle the green spring onion sections on top.

Korean Noodle Stir-fry with Beef and Vegetables

A relatively quick and easy stir-fry, this serves two to three people.

175g/6oz dried egg noodles
175g/6oz sirloin or rump steak (trimmed weight)
1 carrot, scrubbed
1 courgette (zucchino), ends trimmed
50g/2oz Chinese leaf cabbage
50g/2oz spinach
6 mushrooms
3 tbsp corn oil
1 small onion, peeled and coarsely chopped
2 green chilies, seeded, de-pithed and sliced
1 tsp salt
1 tsp sugar
2 tbsp Kikkoman's soy sauce
2 tsp sesame oil

Bring a large pan of water to the boil, add the noodles, and cook until *al dente*, then rinse under cold water and drain.

Meanwhile, thinly slice the beef and cut it into thin strips approximately 5cm/2 inches long and 2cm/3/4 inch wide. Thinly slice the carrot and courgette, then stack the slices and cut them into matchstick strips. Trim off the stalks and coarsely shred the Chinese leaf cabbage and spinach. Thinly slice the mushrooms.

In a wok, heat the oil to smoking point, add the onion and stir-fry for 2 minutes. Add the beef and stir-fry for 1 minute longer, then add all the vegetables and the mushrooms and stir-fry for 2 minutes. Add the salt, sugar, soy sauce and sesame oil. Mix, add the noodles, toss to coat and serve as soon as they have heated through.

Szechwan-style Noodles

These spicy noodles are typical of the popular snacks that are served by street vendors and small neighbourhood food-sellers in China. The crunchy bits of bacon give an excellent flavour and texture, and the chili bean sauce a subtle heat. Serves two; four if accompanied by other dishes.

3 tbsp peanut oil
100g/4oz back bacon, trimmed and finely diced
small piece of fresh ginger, peeled and finely chopped
2 cloves of garlic, peeled and finely chopped
6 spring onions (scallions), trimmed and thinly sliced
1 tsp chili bean sauce
1 tbsp peanut butter
1 tbsp light soy sauce
250ml/8fl oz/1 cup chicken stock/broth (see page 50)
450g/1lb fresh egg 'oil' noodles
2 tsp sesame oil

Heat the oil to smoking point in a wok. Add the bacon and fry until crisp, stirring constantly to prevent burning, then lift with a slotted spoon and drain on absorbent paper; don't worry if a few morsels are left in the oil. Add the ginger, garlic and spring onions and stir-fry for less than a minute. Add the chili bean sauce, peanut butter, soy sauce, and the stock. Bring to the boil and cook down for about 3 minutes, then add the noodles to the wok and toss until well coated and heated through. Turn into a bowl, sprinkle the bacon and sesame oil on top and eat straight away.

Beef-Chili Noodles with Green Pepper

Here, egg noodles are the base for strips of tender marinated beef and cubed green pepper bathed in a fairly mild chili sauce. The fresh coriander gives a warm, spicy scent and flavour. Serves two to three people.

175g/6oz rump or sirloin steak (trimmed weight)
2 tsp Shaohsing wine
3 tbsp light soy sauce
2 tsp sesame oil
freshly ground black pepper
225g/8oz thick or medium, dried egg noodles
2 tsp flour
120ml/4fl oz/1/2 cup water
2 tbsp chili sauce
1 tbsp rice vinegar
2 tbsp peanut oil
2 cloves of garlic, peeled and thinly sliced
1 green pepper, seeded, cored and coarsely chopped
4 spring onions (scallions), trimmed and coarsely sliced
leaves from 6 sprigs of fresh coriander (cilantro), chopped

Cut the beef into small, thin strips, trimming off and discarding the fat. Put in a bowl and add the Shaohsing wine, 1 tbsp light soy sauce, the sesame oil and a generous grinding of black pepper. Mix thoroughly and set aside to marinate for 1 hour.

About 10 minutes before you are ready to start cooking, boil the noodles in a large pot of water until *al dente*, then rinse under cold water and drain. Mix together the flour, water, chili sauce, rice vinegar and the remaining 2 tbsp soy sauce. Stir until all the flour lumps have dissolved. Lift the beef from the marinade with a slotted spoon and drain, discarding the marinade.

Heat the peanut oil to smoking point in a wok. Add the garlic and green pepper and stir-fry for 1 minute, then add the beef and spring onions and stir-fry for 1 minute longer. Stir the chili sauce mixture and pour into the wok. Cook for 1 minute, then add the noodles and toss to coat and heat through. Transfer to a warmed serving dish, scatter the coriander on top, and eat immediately.

Noodles with Peppery Beef and Chili Oil

This is a very hot dish, but you can omit the chili oil altogether and be left with a pleasant, warming peppery taste without any of the fierce chili bite. Mangetouts and mushrooms help to make this a substantial, complete meal for two to three people.

175g/6oz rump or sirloin steak (trimmed
    weight)
freshly ground black pepper
3 tbsp light soy sauce
1 tsp sugar
2 tsp sesame oil
50g/2oz mangetouts (snow peas)
50g/2oz button mushrooms
175g/6oz dried egg noodles
2 tbsp peanut oil
1cm/¹/2 inch piece of fresh ginger, peeled
    and finely chopped
6 small red shallots (or 3 larger yellow
    ones), peeled and sliced
2 tbsp Shaohsing wine
4 tbsp beef stock/broth (see page 49)
    or water
1–2 tsp chili oil (optional)

Slice the steak into thin strips about 5cm/ 2 inches long, put them in a bowl and season with plenty of freshly ground black pepper. Add 1 tbsp light soy sauce, the sugar and the sesame oil, stir to blend and set aside for at least 1 hour. Trim the mangetouts and mushrooms. Stack the mangetouts on a horizontal plane and cut them in half. Quarter the mushrooms.

Boil the egg noodles as directed on the packet or until *al dente*, rinse under cold water and drain. Heat the peanut oil to smoking point in a wok. Lift the beef from the marinade with a slotted spoon, add to the wok and stir-fry for 1 minute longer. Remove and reserve. Add the ginger and shallots and stir fry for 30 seconds, then add the mangetouts and mushrooms and stir-fry for 1 minute. Add the Shaohsing wine, stock or water and the remaining soy sauce. Cook for 1–2 minutes to thicken slightly and add the noodles. Toss to coat and serve as soon as they have heated through, with the chili oil sprinkled on top if desired.

Noodles with Marinated Beef

Morsels of tender marinated beef, mild green chili peppers and broccoli are the main flavouring ingredients of this spicy noodle dish which serves two people as a complete meal.

100g/4oz rump steak (trimmed weight)
6 tbsp peanut oil
1/2 tsp sugar
2 tsp Shaohsing wine
1 tbsp soy sauce
225g/8oz dried egg noodles
100g/4oz broccoli florets
3 cloves of garlic, peeled and finely
  chopped
2.5cm/1 inch piece of fresh ginger, peeled
  and finely chopped
4 large, mild green chillies, seeded and
  coarsely chopped
100g/4oz button mushrooms, thinly sliced
1 tbsp rice vinegar
4 spring onions (scallions), sliced
1 tbsp sesame oil

Slice the beef into thin strips, put in a bowl and combine with 2 tbsp peanut oil and the sugar, wine and soy sauce, stirring well. Set aside.

Bring a large pan of salted water to the boil, add the egg noodles and cook until tender, then rinse under cold water and drain. Bring the water back to the boil and immerse the broccoli for 1 minute. Refresh under cold running water and drain.

Heat the remaining oil in a wok. Add the garlic and ginger, toss in the oil for 30 seconds, then add the chilies. Stir-fry for 30 seconds. Add the mushrooms and broccoli and stir-fry for a minute. Add the beef and its marinade, the rice vinegar and spring onions. Stir-fry for 1 minute longer, then add the noodles and stir-fry for another minute.

Transfer to a hot serving platter and sprinkle the sesame oil over the noodles. Eat straight away.

NOODLE CURRIES

The popularity of 'curries', which I rather imprecisely define as hot, saucy food preparations cooked with a mixture of spices, spread eastwards from the Indian subcontinent and Sri Lanka to Indochina and the Orient, and curried noodles are popular today in both China and Japan. However, it is Thai cooking, which most obviously blends Indian and Chinese influences, that is the inspiration for many of the delicious recipes that follow.

Many of the dishes in this final chapter are adapted from authentic originals, but some, such as my Oriental version of *Pesto noodles* are very inventive and barely qualify as 'curries', even by my own very loose definition, but they are saucy, hot and spicy!

Coconut milk makes fragrant, subtle curry sauces, and when enriched with the excellent commercial brands of curry pastes that are available today, you have the basis for impressive noodle dishes that are both fast to prepare and delicious.

Chilies usually provide the addictive 'heat' in curries, but one dish – *Chicken curry noodles with peppercorns* – preserves the ancient Asian custom of pepping up sauces with indigenous peppercorns. Ironically, chilies were discovered by Europeans seeking to monopolize the trade in pepper, and although alien to Asia, they quickly became popular following their introduction by the Spaniards and Portuguese.

[v] Curried Noodles with Beans, Green Pepper and Bean Curd

This delicious vegetarian noodle curry is cooked in a typically Thai manner. Served with the nutritious garnishes, it is ample for two to three people.

175g/6oz yardlong or green beans, trimmed and cut into 2cm / 3/4 inch lengths
225g/8oz thick, dried egg noodles
3 tbsp corn oil
1 egg plus 1 egg yolk, beaten
1 small green pepper, de-seeded, de-pithed and diced
4 shallots, peeled and finely chopped
3 cloves of garlic, peeled and finely chopped
2 fresh chilies, seeded and thinly sliced
1 tbsp Thai 'green' curry paste
225g/8oz solid bean curd, cut into 2cm/3/4 inch cubes
1 tbsp light soy sauce
1 tbsp dark soy sauce
1 tsp sugar
6 tbsp vegetable stock/broth (see page 51) or water
juice of 1 lime
50g/2oz roasted peanuts, lightly crushed handful of fresh coriander (cilantro), chopped

Bring a large pan of water to the boil, add the beans, return to the boil and blanch for just 30 seconds. Remove the beans with a slotted spoon, refresh under cold running water and drain. Boil the water again, add the noodles, return to the boil and cook until *al dente*. Rinse under cold water, drain and set aside.

In a small, non-stick frying pan heat 1 tbsp oil to smoking point, add the beaten eggs and make an omelette. Drain on absorbent paper and shred coarsely.

Heat the remaining oil to smoking point in a wok. Add the green pepper, shallots, garlic and chilies, stir-fry for 1 minute. Add the curry paste and stir to release aroma, then add the bean curd and green beans and stir-fry for 1 minute longer. Add the soy sauces, sugar and stock. Bring to the boil and cook for 1 minute then add the noodles and toss to coat and heat through. Transfer to a serving platter, arrange the shredded omelette over the noodles, squeeze the lime juice on top, and scatter over the peanuts and coriander. Eat immediately.

v Oriental 'Pesto' Noodles

I created this as a kind of culinary pun, reasoning that the classic Genovese pesto – pasta coated with a green sauce made of fresh basil pounded with pine nuts, olive oil, garlic and cheese – could be reconstructed with Oriental ingredients such as egg noodles, coriander, cashew nuts, peanut oil, spring onions, chilies, ginger and green curry paste. I was very pleasantly surprised by the resulting taste, texture and appearance of the dish. Makes enough for two people.

225g/8oz dried egg noodles
the leaves stripped from a handful of
coriander (cilantro), plus 2 sprigs to
*   garnish*
small handful of sweet basil plus 2 sprigs
*   to garnish*
1 clove of garlic
3 spring onions (scallions), trimmed and
*   chopped*
2–3 fresh chilies, seeded and chopped
small piece of fresh ginger, peeled and
*   chopped*
4 heaped tbsp roasted cashew nuts
6 tbsp peanut oil
2 heaped tsp green masala curry paste
juice of 1 lime or 1/2 lemon
1 tsp sugar
1/2 tsp salt

Boil the noodles until *al dente* or as directed by the packet instructions, then rinse and drain thoroughly. Put the herbs, garlic, spring onions, chilies, ginger, half the cashews, and 5 tbsp peanut oil into a food processor. Blend to a thick paste. Coarsely chop the remaining cashews and reserve them to use as a garnish for the noodles.

Heat the remaining oil in a wok. Fry the paste for 30 seconds to release the aroma, then stir in the curry paste and add the lime or lemon juice, sugar and salt. Stir-fry for 30 seconds longer, then add the noodles and toss to coat thoroughly. Serve as soon as they have heated through, garnished with the reserved cashews and the sprigs of coriander and basil.

Egg Noodle Curry with Vegetables

This recipe makes a steaming platter of delicious fresh egg noodles studded with morsels of tender vegetables curried in coconut milk. The fresh egg noodles will be found only in Oriental supermarkets. However, the other ingredients are all readily available in the larger supermarket branches. This makes a complete light lunch or supper for four, or it will serve six as a starter.

450g/1lb fresh egg noodles
6–8 broccoli florets
12 green beans, trimmed
4 tbsp peanut oil
1 medium aubergine (eggplant), diced
100g/4oz button mushrooms, sliced
2 fresh chilies, washed, seeded and sliced
6–8 small red shallots (or 3–4 yellow
*   shallots), peeled and chopped*
3 cloves of garlic, peeled and finely
*   chopped*
2 tsp Thai 'red' curry paste
300ml/10fl oz/1¹/₄ cups canned coconut
*   milk*
1 tsp sugar
1 tbsp fish sauce (if strictly for vegetarians,
*   replace with dark soy sauce)*
1 tbsp light soy sauce
heart of a crisp lettuce, shredded
handful of fresh coriander (cilantro),
*   washed and chopped*
50g/2oz roasted cashews, roughly chopped
2 hard-boiled (hard-cooked) eggs, shelled
*   and chopped*

Bring a large pan of water to the boil, add the noodles, return to the boil and cook for a few seconds until *al dente*. Rinse and drain.

Lightly par-boil the broccoli and the green beans, then refresh them in cold water and drain well. Divide the florets into small pieces. Cut the beans into 2cm/³/₄ inch lengths.

Heat the oil to smoking point in a wok. Add the vegetables and stir-fry for a minute. Add the chilies, shallots and garlic, and stir-fry for a minute longer. Stir the curry paste into the vegetables and pour in the coconut milk. Add the sugar, and the fish and soy sauces. Mix well and add the noodles. Toss these in the sauce for about 2 minutes, to heat through, and transfer to a warmed serving platter, surrounding the noodles with the shredded lettuce. Sprinkle with the coriander, cashews and hard-boiled eggs. Serve immediately.

Three-Mushroom Curried Noodles

For this Thai-inspired noodle curry I have used fresh and dried shiitake, as well as fresh oyster and button mushrooms, but for the latter you could substitute canned paddy-straw mushrooms, if you can find them. It makes a delicious and complete vegetarian meal for two to three people.

225g/8oz dried, thread egg noodles
15g/¹/₂oz dried shiitake mushrooms
25g/1oz fresh shiitake mushrooms
50g/2oz oyster mushrooms
50g/2oz button mushrooms
4 tbsp peanut oil
3 shallots, peeled and chopped
3 cloves of garlic, peeled and thinly sliced
1 stick (stalk) of lemon grass, very thinly sliced
1 tbsp Thai 'red' curry paste
3 fresh chilies, seeded and thinly sliced
1 tbsp light soy sauce
1 tbsp fish sauce (if strictly for vegetarians, replace with dark soy sauce)
2 tsp sugar
1 tsp salt
grated peel and juice of 1 lime
250ml/8fl oz/1 cup canned coconut milk
50g/2oz bean sprouts
6 sprigs of holy basil or 12 sweet basil leaves
¹/₂ large cucumber, peeled and thinly sliced

Boil the noodles according to the packet instructions. Rinse, drain and reserve them. Soak the dried shiitake mushrooms in a cup of hot water for 30 minutes. Strain and reserve the soaking liquid. Remove and discard the tough stalks and slice the caps as thinly as possible. Chop the fresh mushrooms coarsely.

Heat the oil in a wok to smoking point. Add the shallots, garlic and lemon grass and stir-fry for 1 minute. Add the curry paste, mix well, and stir-fry for 30 seconds, then add the mushrooms and chilies. Stir-fry for 1 minute, then add the soy and fish sauces, sugar and salt. Stir, and add the lime peel and juice.

Stir, and pour in the strained mushroom soaking liquid. Reduce by half, then add the coconut milk and the noodles. Turn the noodles in the sauce for about 2¹/₂ minutes, or until the curry has thickened and reduced in volume by one third.

Mix in the bean sprouts, cook for a few seconds longer and transfer to a shallow serving dish. Scatter the basil on top and serve, surrounded by a ring of overlapping cucumber slices.

Hot, Sweet and Sour Noodles

Use fresh, thin wheat or egg noodles for this savoury curry. It is quite a hot dish, but the chili sauce can be reduced to just 1/2 tsp or omitted altogether. Serves three people.

8 dried shiitake mushrooms
450g/1lb fresh, thin wheat or egg noodles
120ml/4fl oz/1/2 cup chicken stock/broth
    (see page 50)
3 tbsp peanut oil
2 small red onions, peeled and chopped
50g/2oz smoked ham, cut into small, thin
    strips
11/2 tsp good curry powder
1 tbsp rice vinegar
3 tsp sugar
1/2 tsp salt
1/4–1/2 tsp cayenne
3 fresh or canned tomatoes, chopped
    (peeled if fresh)
1 tbsp light soy sauce
11/2 tsp hoisin sauce
1 tsp chili sauce

Soak the shiitake mushrooms for 30 minutes in a teacup of hot water. Meanwhile bring abundant water to the boil, add the noodles, return to the boil and, separating the strands, boil for 30 seconds longer. Rinse under cold water and drain.

Remove the mushrooms, strain their soaking liquid and add it to the chicken stock. Discard the mushrooms' tough stems and thinly slice the caps.

Heat the oil to smoking point in a wok. Add the onions, ham and mushroom strips and stir-fry for 2–3 minutes. Add the curry powder, stir, then add the vinegar, sugar, salt, cayenne and tomatoes. Stir and cook the mixture for 2 minutes longer. Stir in the soy, hoisin and chili sauces, and pour in the stock. Bring to the boil, cook for 2 minutes, then add the noodles and serve as soon as the noodles have heated through.

Fresh Egg Noodle Curry with Prawns

This recipe makes a luscious and fragrant 'red' curry. Fresh ribbon egg noodles are rather like Italian fettuccine or tagliatelle, and their texture goes very well with the soupy curry sauce. Serves four.

350g/12oz fresh egg ribbon noodles
3 tbsp peanut oil
2 lemon grass sticks (stalks), trimmed and
    thinly sliced
1 large carrot, scrubbed and finely diced
3 cloves of garlic, peeled and finely
    chopped
8 small red or 3–4 yellow shallots, peeled
    and sliced into thin rings
3 tsp Thai 'red' curry paste
2 kaffir lime leaves, thinly sliced
400ml/14fl oz/1 3/4 cups canned coconut
    milk
120ml/4fl oz/1/2 cup water
juice of 1/2 lemon
1 tbsp light soy sauce
1 tbsp fish sauce
1/4–1/2 tsp cayenne
1 tsp sugar
225g/8oz peeled, cooked tiger prawns
    (shrimp), thawed if frozen
2 fresh chilies, seeded and thinly sliced
1 'little gem' lettuce, shredded
small handful of fresh coriander (cilantro),
    chopped

Bring abundant water to the boil, add the noodles, return to the boil and cook for 1–2 minutes or until just *al dente*. Drain, toss in 1 tbsp oil and put the noodles into a serving bowl. Keep warm in a cool oven; they should not 'cook'.

Heat the remaining oil to smoking point in a wok, add the lemon grass, carrot, garlic and shallots and stir-fry for 1 minute, then add the curry paste and lime leaves and stir-fry for 30 seconds longer. Pour in the coconut milk, water, lemon juice, and the soy and fish sauces. Stir in the cayenne and sugar, bring to the boil, then reduce the heat slightly and simmer for about 6 minutes or until the sauce has thickened slightly. Add the prawns, chilies, lettuce and coriander to the curry and mix to heat through. Meanwhile, separate the noodle strands with your hands, disentangling any clumps. Pour the contents of the wok over the noodles and eat straight away.

Egg Curry Noodles

Eggs and curry sauces combine very successfully, and in this attractive, easy dish their flavour is enhanced by the crisp bacon garnish. Ready-made curry paste simplifies the preparation, but do use a good brand such as *Patak's* or *Fern's*. This makes a complete light lunch or supper for two to three people.

450g/1lb fresh udon or egg 'oil' noodles
3 tbsp corn oil
1 red onion, peeled, halved from top to
    bottom, and thinly sliced
4 cloves of garlic, peeled and finely
    chopped
5cm/2 inch piece of fresh ginger, peeled
    and finely chopped
50g/2oz blanched, flaked almonds, lightly
    toasted
1 tsp cayenne
1 tsp turmeric
2 large, dried red chilies, coarsely sliced
1 tbsp Indian curry paste
4 tbsp water
175ml/6fl oz/³/₄ cup canned coconut milk
salt and freshly ground black pepper
6 hard-boiled (hard-cooked) eggs, peeled
    and quartered
small handful of fresh coriander (cilantro),
    chopped
2 slices crisply grilled bacon, finely diced
    or shredded (optional)

Bring a large pan of water to the boil, add the *udon* noodles, return to the boil and cook for 1 minute, then rinse under cold water and drain. (Omit this step if you are using egg 'oil' noodles.)

Heat the oil to smoking point in a wok, add the onion and fry for 2 minutes, then add the garlic, ginger, flaked almonds, cayenne, turmeric and chilies. Stir for 15 seconds, then add the curry paste, stir for a few seconds to release aroma, then pour in the water. Heat for 1 minute or until the mixture thickens, then pour in the coconut milk, season, reduce the heat and simmer for 10–15 minutes or until the sauce is thick and luscious. Add the noodles, mix, moisten with a splash of water if necessary and cover the wok. Heat through for 2–3 minutes longer, then transfer the wok contents to a serving platter, surround the noodles with the quartered eggs, sprinkle with coriander and bacon, and eat straight away.

Noodles with Spicy Shredded Chicken Curry

Here the noodles are coated in a delicious shredded chicken curry, redolent of coconut milk and a medley of Thai flavourings. Fresh egg 'oil' noodles have just the right plump, soft texture, but dried egg noodles, suitably boiled, rinsed and drained may be substituted.
Serves two to four people.

*1 skinned chicken breast or the meat from
    2 chicken legs*
*350ml/12fl oz/1¹/2 cups canned coconut
    milk*
2 tbsp peanut oil
*3 cloves of garlic, peeled and finely
    chopped*
*white part of 4 spring onions (scallions),
    finely chopped*
*2.5cm/1 inch piece of fresh ginger, peeled
    and finely chopped*
1 carrot, peeled and very finely chopped
3 fresh chilies, seeded and finely chopped
2 tsp Thai 'red' curry paste
¹/2 tsp turmeric
freshly ground black pepper
1 tbsp soy sauce
1 tbsp fish sauce
2 tsp rice vinegar
3 tbsp roasted peanuts, crushed
450g/1lb fresh egg 'oil' noodles
*handful of fresh coriander (cilantro),
    finely chopped*

Put the chicken breast and coconut milk into a pan and simmer for 15–20 minutes, turning a few times. Remove the chicken breast, allow to cool a little, then shred, not too finely. Save the coconut milk.

Heat the peanut oil in a wok or non-stick frying pan. Add the chicken, garlic, spring onions, ginger, carrot and chilies, stir-fry for 1 minute, then add the curry paste, turmeric and a generous grinding of black pepper. Stir-fry for 1 minute more, then add the soy and fish sauces, vinegar, crushed peanuts, and the reserved coconut milk. Stir until thick – this will just take 30–60 seconds. Add the noodles, toss to coat and heat through, sprinkle the coriander on top and serve straight away.

v Noodle 'Cake' with Curried Vegetables

This form of curried vegetables is closer to Indian versions than to south-east Asian curries, and makes a spicy topping for a fried noodle 'cake'. Once the curry base has been made it may be refrigerated in a sealed container for up to three days or frozen, making this a convenient and quick standby. The curry also makes an excellent filling for samosas and may even be used to stuff filo pastry parcels, which should then be fried. Serves two to three people.

225g/8oz dried egg noodles
1cm/¹/₂ inch piece of cinnamon
3 cloves
1 tsp cumin seeds
1 tsp coriander seeds
450g/1lb salad potatoes, peeled and boiled
*   until just tender*
sunflower oil for frying the noodle 'cake'
*   plus 3 tbsp*
1 small onion, peeled and finely chopped
1 carrot, peeled and finely chopped
1 stick (stalk) of celery, thinly sliced
3 cloves of garlic, peeled and finely
*   chopped*
1cm/¹/₂ inch piece of fresh ginger, peeled
*   and finely chopped*
2 fresh chilies, seeded and finely chopped
1 tsp turmeric
salt and freshly ground black pepper
100g/4oz peas, thawed if frozen
225g/8oz canned tomatoes, chopped
generous handful of fresh coriander
*   (cilantro), finely chopped*

Bring abundant water to the boil, add the noodles, separate the strands and cook until *al dente*, then rinse under cold water, drain very thoroughly, and pat dry with absorbent paper to remove all traces of moisture. Meanwhile, heat a clean, seasoned frying pan without oil, add the cinnamon, cloves, cumin and coriander and stir until they release aroma and the seeds start to pop. Remove the spices and grind them in a clean coffee grinder or pound to a coarse powder with a pestle and mortar. Dice the potatoes.

Heat about 7 tbsp oil to smoking point in a wok, add the noodles and press them down with a spatula to make a thick layer. Fry until the base is golden-brown but not burnt, then loosen, turn and fry the other side until golden-brown.

Remove the noodle 'cake' with a spatula, scrape away any debris and wipe the wok clean. Keep the noodles warm on a serving platter lined with absorbent paper, which should be removed once the noodles are well-drained.

Heat 3 tbsp oil in the wok and sauté the onion, carrot and celery until golden, then add the garlic, ginger and chilies. Stir-fry for about 2 minutes, then add the ground spices and turmeric. Season, add the cooked potatoes, peas, tomatoes and 120ml/4fl oz/$\frac{1}{2}$ cup water. Bring to the boil and cook, uncovered, until the mixture has thickened slightly (3–4 minutes longer). Stir in the coriander and spread the curry over the noodle cake. Eat straight away.

Chicken Curry Noodles with Peppercorns

This delicious curry derives its pungent heat from peppercorns, not chilies. The Thai island of Koh-Samui is famed both for its coconut groves and for the luxuriant pepper vines that grow profusely up the slender trunks of the palms. Until the Portuguese brought chilies to this part of Asia from their enclave in Goa, pepper provided the heat. Once introduced to chilies, the Thais took to their fiercer heat like ducks to water! You can crush the peppercorns with a pestle and mortar or in a coffee grinder. Serves two to three people.

450g/1lb fresh egg noodles
1 large chicken breast, skinned
3 tsp mixed peppercorns, crushed
1 tbsp plain (all-purpose) flour
2 tbsp peanut oil
2 cloves of garlic, peeled and thinly sliced
2–3 tsp Thai 'green' curry paste
250ml/8fl oz/1 cup canned coconut milk
juice of 1 lime
2–3 tsp fish sauce
1 tbsp light soy sauce
2 tsp sugar
50g/2oz roasted peanuts, lightly crushed
handful of holy basil or sweet basil sprigs

Bring a large pan of water to the boil, add the noodles, return to the heat and cook until *al dente*. Rinse under cold water and drain.

Cut the chicken into even cubes each about 3cm/1¼ inches square. Roll them first in the pepper, then in the flour. Heat the oil to smoking point in a wok. Add the chicken pieces and garlic and stir-fry for 15–30 seconds or until lightly coloured, then add the curry paste and stir-fry for a few seconds longer. Pour in all the liquids, and add the sugar and peanuts. Stir the mixture for about 2 minutes or until it thickens slightly, then add the noodles and basil and toss to coat and heat through. Transfer to a warmed serving dish and eat immediately.

Chicken Noodle Curry with Potatoes

If the notion of adding potatoes to noodles seems excessively starchy, think of the true Genovese pesto, a dish that combines pasta with boiled potatoes, and sometimes green beans, dressed in the eponymous raw basil sauce. This curry is a wonderful noodle dish, richly redolent of Thailand, and an ample serving for two to three people.

175g/6oz thick, dried egg noodles
225g/8oz small salad potatoes, peeled and
    halved
100g/4oz bean sprouts
1 small, slender or 3 baby aubergines
    (eggplant), trimmed
3 tbsp peanut oil
3 cloves of garlic, peeled and finely
    chopped
2cm/3/4 inch piece of fresh ginger, peeled
    and finely chopped
2 fresh chilies, seeded and finely chopped
175g/6oz skinless, boned chicken breast
    meat, cut into thumbnail-size pieces
1 tbsp Thai 'red' curry paste
400ml/14fl oz/1 3/4 cups canned coconut
    milk
juice of 1/2 lemon
1 tbsp fish sauce
1 tbsp light soy sauce
3 kaffir lime leaves, thinly sliced
2 tsp sugar
small handful of fresh or holy basil
1/4–1/2 tsp Thai 7-spice mixture (optional)

Bring a large pan of salted water to the boil. Add the noodles, stir to separate the strands, and boil until *al dente*, then, saving their cooking water, rinse the noodles under cold water and drain. Return the water to the boil, add the potatoes and boil until just tender. Drain and set aside. Put the noodles in the bottom of a large serving bowl or soup tureen and arrange the bean sprouts on top. Cut the aubergines into thumbnail-size cubes.

Heat the oil to smoking point in a wok. Fry the garlic, ginger and chilies for a few seconds, add the chicken pieces and stir-fry for 30 seconds, then add the aubergines and stir-fry for 30 seconds longer. Add the curry paste, mix to release aroma and pour in the coconut milk, lemon juice, the fish and soy sauces. Add the potatoes, lime leaves and sugar, and bring to the boil. Reduce the heat slightly and let the curry bubble for about 6 minutes. Add the basil and pour the curry over the noodles. Dust with 7-spice mixture, if desired, and eat straight away.

Chicken Satay with Rice or Noodles

I happened upon an excellent leftovers dish when I had some surplus grilled chicken *satay* and a small amount of the spicy peanut sauce that goes so well with it. Since I invariably serve *satay* as a light lunch dish, with plenty of starch (boiled rice) to soak up the delicious peanut sauce, why not combine it with noodles? I give first the main *satay* recipe, including the traditional accompanying salad, so that you can enjoy that, with or without a plain rice or noodle accompaniment; you can then use up the leftovers in a noodle dish the next day. If you just want the *satay* noodles, make up one quarter the quantities of the *satay* and peanut sauce, which will combine with 225g/8oz dried egg noodles to give you two to four servings.

4 chicken breasts
4 cloves of garlic, peeled and crushed
2cm/3/4 inch piece of ginger, peeled and
    finely chopped
2 tbsp peanut oil
4 tbsp single (light) cream or Greek yoghurt
1 tbsp very fresh garam masala
1 tsp cayenne
1 tsp turmeric
1 tbsp light soy sauce
1 tbsp fish sauce
salt and freshly ground black pepper
juice of 1/2 lemon

Skin the chicken breasts and slice them into strips about 1cm/1/2 inch wide. Put them into a bowl and add the remaining ingredients. Mix thoroughly, cover, and leave to marinate for at least 1 hour.

Peanut Sauce

☑ Carrot and Cucumber Salad

4 tbsp peanut oil
4 tbsp peanut oil
1 small onion, peeled and finely chopped
2 cloves of garlic, peeled and finely
  chopped
4 heaped tbsp crunchy peanut butter
4 tbsp coconut milk
250ml/8fl oz/1 cup water
1 tbsp sugar
1 tsp cayenne
1 tsp turmeric
1 tbsp fish sauce
1 tbsp light soy sauce

While the chicken marinates make the peanut sauce. Heat the oil and fry the onion and garlic. Before they brown, add the peanut butter and fry for about 1 minute longer, then add the remaining ingredients, mix well, and simmer until the sauce darkens a shade and the oil has started to separate.

When ready to start the *satay* thread the chicken slices on to skewers, then grill (broil), barbecue, or char-grill on a hot, dry griddle, turning a few times to ensure all sides are a dark golden-brown. While cooking, baste each side once with the remaining marinade, which makes a crust and keeps the chicken exceptionally tender. Serve the peanut sauce and the carrot and cucumber salad in separate bowls and, if desired, with boiled rice or noodles.

My version of the sweet, sour and salty salad that traditionally accompanies *satay*.

¹/₂ cucumber, peeled, washed and halved
2 medium carrots, scrubbed, halved from
  top to bottom, and very thinly sliced
2 tbsp sugar
2 tbsp rice vinegar
1 tbsp light soy sauce
1 fresh chili, seeded and thinly sliced into
  long strips
leaves from 6 sprigs of coriander (cilantro),
  chopped
50g/2oz roasted peanuts, crushed

Remove the seedy centre from the cucumber with a teaspoon and discard it. Slice the flesh very thinly and mix together with the carrots in a bowl. Put the sugar, vinegar and soy sauce in a small enamelled or stainless steel saucepan and bring to a simmer, stirring to dissolve the sugar granules. Remove from the heat, and when cooled pour the liquid over the vegetables. Sprinkle with the chilies, coriander and peanuts.

Satay Noodles

For this you will need one chicken breast, prepared and cooked as in the main *satay* recipe, and approximately 120ml/4fl oz/ 1/2 cup of the cooked peanut sauce. Serve with an accompanying carrot and cucumber salad. As this is quite rich, the serving quantity is for three to four people.

225g/8oz dried egg noodles
1 grilled chicken satay skewer
250ml/8fl oz/1 cup cooked peanut sauce, diluted with a little water
2 tbsp peanut oil
3 shallots, peeled and finely chopped
1/2 sweet red pepper, seeded, de-pithed and finely diced
2 tsp Thai 'green' or Indian 'green masala' curry paste
1 tbsp light soy sauce
1 tsp sugar
4 tbsp canned coconut milk
juice of 1/2 lemon
leaves from 6 sprigs of fresh coriander (cilantro), chopped

Boil the noodles in abundant water until *al dente*, rinse and drain. Take the chicken pieces off the skewer and halve or quarter them. In a small pan, re-heat the peanut sauce, diluted with just a little water. When it bubbles, turn off the heat but cover the pan to keep the sauce warm.

Heat the oil to smoking point in a wok, add the shallots and red pepper and stir-fry for 1 1/2 minutes. Add the curry paste and stir to release aroma. Add the soy sauce and sugar, mix, then add the peanut sauce, chicken, coconut milk and lemon juice. Let the sauce bubble for 2 minutes, add the noodles and toss to coat and heat through. Transfer to a warmed serving dish and scatter the coriander on top. Eat straight away.

Beef Curry Noodles

A delicious Thai curry, which I like very sour with fresh lime juice; just use the juice from 1 lime for a less tart curry. The addition of plump fresh rice or wheat noodles transforms this into a complete one-wok meal, which serves three to four people.

450g/1lb fresh thick rice or wheat noodles
175g/6oz rump steak (trimmed weight)
2 tbsp peanut oil
3 cloves of garlic, peeled and thinly sliced
75g/3oz sliced bamboo shoots (canned ones are fine), rinsed and drained
1 tbsp Thai 'green' curry paste
1/2–1 tsp cayenne
1 tbsp light soy sauce
1 tbsp fish sauce
juice of 1 or 2 limes, to taste
1 tsp sugar
400ml/14fl oz/1 3/4 cups canned coconut milk
small handful of holy basil or sweet basil leaves

Bring a large pan of water to the boil, add the fresh noodles, return to the boil and cook briefly until just *al dente*. Rinse the noodles under cold water and drain. Slice the beef into thin strips.

Heat the oil to smoking point in a wok. Add the garlic and beef and stir-fry for 1 minute, then add the bamboo shoots, the curry paste and the cayenne. Stir-fry for 30 seconds, then add the soy and fish sauces, the lime juice and sugar. Mix, then pour in the coconut milk. Bring to the boil and cook, stirring often, until the curry thickens appreciably: this will take from 8–15 minutes. Add the basil and the noodles, toss to coat and heat through. Turn on to a warmed serving dish and eat straight away.

Rich Beef Masala with Almonds and Noodles

For best results, make this superb curry in advance and re-heat it the following day; that way the flavour will intensify. Patak's make a very good brand of green masala curry paste but you can substitute any other quality brand. This rich noodle dish serves two to three people.

350g/12oz good stewing steak, trimmed
of fat
1 small onion, peeled
3 cloves of garlic, peeled and quartered
2cm/3/4 inch piece of fresh ginger, peeled
and sliced
2 fresh, green chilies
50g/2oz blanched, flaked almonds, lightly
toasted
2 tbsp corn oil
salt and freshly ground black pepper
3 tbsp water plus extra water for
moistening the curry
120ml/4fl oz/1/2 cup canned coconut milk
· 1/2 tbsp Indian green masala curry paste
120ml/4floz/1/2 cup beef stock/broth
(see page 49)
juice of 1/2 lemon
1 tsp sugar
1 tsp salt
175g/6oz dried, medium egg noodles

Cut the beef into 2cm/1/2 inch chunks. Put into a blender the onion, garlic, ginger, chilies, almonds, oil, seasoning, and 3 tbsp water. Blend to a paste.

Heat a medium-sized pan or casserole, add the freshly-made paste and stir-fry vigorously for about 3 minutes. Pour in the coconut milk, stir in the green masala curry paste and add the stock, lemon juice, sugar and salt. Bring to the boil, add the beef, then reduce the heat, cover the pan tightly and simmer over the gentlest heat for 1 1/2 hours, stirring and adding more water from time to time to prevent the curry from drying out and burning. Remove from the heat and reserve.

When nearly ready to eat, bring a large pan of water to the boil, add the noodles, return to the boil, separating the strands, and cook until al dente. Drain.

Re-heat the curry, add the noodles and heat through, mixing well. Serve as hot as possible.

Singapore Curried Noodles

There are many versions of 'Singapore' noodles. One, made without curry spices, will be found on page 102. This one is quite hot and spicy, and serves three people.

175g/6oz fresh, raw or cooked, peeled tiger
    prawns/shrimp (properly thawed if
    frozen)
1/2 tsp salt
a few drops of Tabasco, or to taste
225g/8oz thin rice noodles ('vermicelli')
3 tbsp peanut oil
2 eggs, beaten
1 small green pepper, seeded, de-pithed
    and diced
1 carrot, scrubbed and finely diced
6 spring onions (scallions), sliced, the
    white and green parts separated
3 cloves of garlic, peeled and finely
    chopped
75g/3oz lean, minced (ground) pork
1 tsp curry powder
1/4 tsp turmeric
1/4 tsp cayenne, or to taste
4 tbsp water
2 tbsp light soy sauce
1/2 tsp sugar
50g/2oz bean sprouts

Put the prawns into a small bowl. Sprinkle with salt and Tabasco and set aside for approximately 30 minutes. Boil the rice noodles in abundant water until just *al dente*, rinse in cold water and drain. Unless you intend to proceed immediately, toss the noodles in a little oil to prevent them from sticking together.

Heat 1 tbsp oil to smoking point in a wok. Add the beaten egg, make an omelette, remove and drain on absorbent paper. Cut into thin strips.

Add 2 tbsp oil to the wok, heat to smoking point, add the raw prawns and stir until pink. Remove and drain. (Keep cooked prawns for a later step.) Add the green pepper and carrot and stir-fry for 1 minute, followed by the white part of the spring onions and the garlic; stir-fry for 30 seconds longer. Add the minced pork and stir-fry for 1 minute or until no longer pink, then add the curry powder, turmeric and cayenne and mix. Return the prawns (or add the cooked ones to the wok, if you are using them). Add the water, soy sauce, sugar and beansprouts, mix, then add the noodles. Toss to coat and heat through thoroughly, then transfer to a warmed serving dish, scatter the omelette strips and the green part of the spring onions over the noodles, and eat straight away.

Thai-style Curried Noodles

Although singing with typically Thai flavourings (hot, sour, sweet and salty) and made with Thai ribbon rice noodles, this delicious recipe is just one of many variations on the popular noodle curries that come from all the south-east Asian countries. It is quite substantial and will serve three to four people.

175g/6oz dried, ribbon rice noodles
400ml/14fl oz/1³/4 cups canned coconut
　　milk
100g/4oz minced (ground) pork
3 cloves of garlic, peeled and thinly sliced
2 kaffir lime leaves, thinly sliced
75g/3oz solid bean curd, diced
1 tbsp yellow or brown bean sauce
1 tbsp good curry powder
1 tbsp sugar
3 fresh chilies, seeded and thinly sliced
100g/4oz peeled cooked prawns (shrimp),
　　thawed if frozen
the crisp inner leaves from a Cos (romaine)
　　lettuce
2 tbsp peanut oil
1 red onion, peeled, halved from top to
　　bottom and thinly sliced
100g/4oz bean sprouts
1 tbsp fish sauce
juice of ¹/2 lemon
1 egg plus 1 egg yolk, beaten
6cm/2¹/2 inch piece of cucumber, peeled,
　　halved from end to end and thinly
　　sliced
small handful of fresh coriander (cilantro),
　　chopped

1 spring onion (scallion), thinly sliced
¹/4–¹/2 tsp cayenne
1 lime, quartered

Bring a large pan of water to the boil, add the noodles, remove from the heat and leave to soak for a minute or until *al dente*. Rinse under cold water and drain.

Put into a hot wok the coconut milk, pork, garlic, lime leaves, bean curd, bean sauce, curry powder and sugar. Mix, bring to the boil, then reduce the heat and simmer for about 15 minutes or until the pork is tender and the sauce has thickened somewhat. Add the chilies and prawns, heat for 1 minute and set aside. Line a serving dish with the lettuce leaves.

Heat the oil to smoking point in a large pan or another wok. Add the onion and stir-fry for 1¹/2 minutes, then add the noodles, bean sprouts, fish sauce, lemon juice, and the beaten egg. Stir-fry for about 2 minutes, then spread the noodle mixture over the lettuce. Briefly re-heat the curry and pour it over the noodles. Garnish with the cucumber, coriander, spring onion, cayenne, and lime quarters. Serve immediately.

ABOUT THE AUTHOR

John Midgley was born in Singapore of English and Spanish parents, lived there for seven years, then moved to Trinidad, Spain and England, where he was educated at Worth Abbey and Trinity College, Oxford. An enthusiastic self-taught cook, he makes daily creative use of fresh seasonal ingredients to feed family and friends. John has worked as a marketing consultant, part-time university lecturer, food writer, and book packager, and is currently a cookery book editor. A finalist in the 1991 Observer Mouton Cadet cookery competition, he is also a member of The Guild of Food Writers and the author of several books including, for Pavilion, *The Goodness of...*series and *100 Great Snacks*.

ACKNOWLEDGEMENTS

I would like to thank Sue, my wife, for all her help and support in the preparation of this book. I would also like to thank James Murphy for his cover photograph, Andrew Farmer for his illustrations, Bet Ayer for designing the book, and Rachel King for tolerating so good naturedly my late delivery.

SELECT BIBLIOGRAPHY

A Taste of the Far East, by Madhur Jaffrey
(Pavilion and BBC, 1993)

Classic Food of China, by Yan-kit So
(Macmillan, 1992)

Eastern Vegetarian Cooking, by Madhur
Jaffrey (Jonathan Cape, 1983)

Indonesian and Thai Cooking, by Sri
Owen (Piatkus, 1988)

Japanese Cooking, A Simple Art, by Shizuo
Tsuji (Kodansha, 1980)

Ken Hom's Chinese Cookery (BBC, 1984)

Ken Hom's Chinese Kitchen (Pavilion, 1994)

Ken Hom's Vegetable and Pasta Book
(BBC, 1987)

Madhur Jaffrey's Far Eastern Cookery
(BBC, 1989)

Oriental Flavours, by Frances Bissell
(Pavilion, 1990)

Real Thai, by Nancy McDermott (Chronicle
Books, 1992)

South East Asian Food, by Rosemary
Brissenden (Penguin, 1970)

Thai Cooking, by Jennifer Brennan (Jill
Norman and Hobhouse, 1981)

Thai Cuisine, by Mogens Esbensen (Nelson
Publishers, 1986)

The Book of Soba, by James Udesky
(Kodansha, 1988)

*The Cookery of Thailand, Indonesia and
Malaysia*, by Sri Owen
(Martin Books for Sainsbury's, 1991)

The Fine Art of Japanese Cooking, by
Hideo Dekura (Bay Books, 1984)

The Korean Kitchen, by Copeland Marks
(Chronicle Books, 1993)

The Taste of China, by Ken Hom (Pavilion,
1990)

The Taste of Thailand, by Vatcharin
Bhumichitr (Pavilion, 1988)

Vatch's Thai Cookbook, by Vatcharin
Bhumichitr (Pavilion, 1994)

Yan-kit's Classic Chinese Cookbook
(Dorling Kindersley, 1984)

MAIL-ORDER SOURCE LIST

There are too many Chinese and Oriental supermarkets around the country to list here. Most large cities have at least one, but in London's Chinatown they proliferate. I count among my favourites:

London

Loon Fung Supermarket Ltd
42 Gerrard Street
London W1 7LP
Loon Moon Supermarket Ltd
9 Gerrard Street
London W1V 7LJ

Golden Gate Chinese Supermarket
14 Lisle Street
London WC2H 7BE

Newport Supermarket
32 Newport Court
London WC2H 7PQ

Good Harvest Fish and Meat Market
Newport Court
London WC2

See Woo Chinese Supermarket
19 Lisle Street
London WC2H 7BE

Yaohan Plaza
399 Edgware Road
Colindale
London NW9 0JJ
(and also by mail order on 0181 200 0009)

Manchester

Wing Yip Supermarket
Thompson Street
Off Oldham Row
Ancoats
Manchester M4 5HU

Birmingham

Wing Yip Supermarket
375 Nuchells Park Road
Nuchells
Birmingham B7 5NT

Glasgow

Chung Ying Supermarket
254 Dobbies Loan
Glasgow G4 0HS

INDEX